MOVING BEYOND THE COUNTER: ELEVATING INTO HEART-CENTERED HEALTH CARE THROUGH ENTREPRENEURSHIP

A Guide for Healers in Health Care to Monetize Your Gifts and own Your Brilliance to Scale Your Profitable Heart-Centered Business

Dr. Christina Fontana, PharmD, CHC, CHt

Enlightened Wellness Solutions Publishing

Pittsburgh, PA

MOVING BEYOND THE COUNTER: ELEVATING INTO HEART-CENTERED HEALTH CARE THROUGH ENTREPRENEURSHIP

A guide for healers in healthcare to monetize your gifts and own your brilliance to scale your profitable heart-centered business.

Copyright © 2022 by Christina Fontana

Printed in the United States of America

Edited and Formatted by: Cori Wamsley, Aurora Corialis Publishing

Cover Design: Karen Captline, BetterBe Creative

Foreword by: Todd Eury

Contributors: Sarah Anderson, Marina Buksov, Jenna Carmichael, Lauren Castle, Nina Castle, Angela Cates, Anh Evardo, Trish Francetich, Melissa Hetrick, Johnnie Kemp, Jennifer Marquez, Sarah Meyers, Angela Orr, Beth Thomas, Melissa Thompson, Katie Wood, Elisabeth Wygant, Mariam Yanikyan, Lisa Zielbauer

Paperback ISBN: 9798845814777

DISCLAIMER

Dr. Christina along with all of the contributors of this book are not medical doctors, therapists, dieticians, or nutritionists. We make no claims to cure, diagnose, or treat any disease. This book is meant to serve as an educational tool to guide you to feel empowered in your life. Please consult with your doctor if you have any questions about starting a new supplement, exercise, therapy, treatment, or herbal regimen.

Although the publisher and the authors have made every effort to ensure that the information in this book was correct at press time and while this publication is designed to provide accurate information in regard to the subject matter covered, the publisher and the authors assume no responsibility for errors, inaccuracies, omissions, or any other inconsistencies and herein and hereby disclaim any liability to any party for any loss, damage, or disruption caused by errors or omissions, whether such errors or omissions result from negligence, accident, or any other cause.

The publisher and the authors make no guarantees concerning the level of success you may experience by following the advice and strategies contained in this book, and you accept the risk that results will differ for each individual.

WITH LOVE

Thank you to my family for being the training ground for my awakening into the heart-centered healer I am today.

Thank you to my husband, Eric, for being my biggest supporter and best friend.

Thank you to my assistants Rachel and Priscilla for supporting the organization of this project.

Thank you to Todd Eury for his unwavering support of my business and mission and for amplifying the voices of thousands of pharmacists through the pharmacy podcast network.

Thank you to the incredible 19 women who graciously and generously contributed to this book to share their inspiring stories.

TABLE OF CONTENTS

How to Get the Most out of this Book i

Foreword v

Introduction 1

Awakening and Unlocking Your Inner Heart-Centered Healer........................7

The New Paradigm for Healing in Health Care....................................21

My Journey of Healing through the Heart..29

Step #1. Unlocking Your Rare and Regal Soul Gifts + Becoming the Queen of Your Business...43

Step #2. Overcoming Self-Sabotage to Feel Safe to Shine 59

Step #3. Releasing Money Memories to Receive Abundantly for Your Gifts......71

Step #4. Communicating and Delivering Your Brilliance to Call in Your Soul Clients..79

Step #5. Systems, Structure, Support to Scale Your Profitable Business 91

Stories of Heart-Centered Healers in Health Care 101

Holistic Health Coaching 102

Personalized Medicine..135

Functional Medicine..140

Financial Coaching 153

Health + Lifestyle Coaching 157

Spiritual Life Coaching 179

Conclusion...185

Integrating This into Your Life 187

How to Get the Most out of this Book

1. **Join our Facebook community.** First, I'd love to connect with you and have you join our Monetize Your Magic Facebook community at www.bitly.com/monetizeyourmagicgroup. You'll be connected to a loving, supportive network of pharmacist entrepreneurs monetizing their gifts, including all of the featured contributors of this book.

2. **I respect your spiritual beliefs.** I will use the terms "God," "Divine," and "Source," and you can feel free to insert what feels most aligned for you and your beliefs. I honor and respect your religious and spiritual beliefs and do not intend to impress my beliefs onto you.

3. **Focus on your unique journey.** If you come across a concept or a story about one of my clients that triggers you, be gentle with yourself. Everyone is at a different stage and place, and the last thing I want you to do is judge or compare yourself.

4. **Be open.** Many of the concepts in this book may be new to you. I encourage you to remain open and release any preconceived notions you may have. That is how you will glean the most from this book.

5. **Take what works and leave the rest.** You may not agree with me on everything in this book. I present a broad scope of information, so you can choose which tools resonate for you and your lifestyle, beliefs, and journey. That's okay! Adapt what works for you, and leave the rest.

6. **Claim the BONUS Step into Your Queen: Scaling Your Heart-Centered Business Trainings + Workbook Bundle to deepen your experience.**

In this BONUS content, you'll find the trainings and PDF guide with:
- Over 40+ subconscious programming audios to help you step into your Queen embodiment
- Specific journal prompts to support you in releasing blocks keeping you stuck

- Energetic management tools to calm your nervous system to feel safe to receive
- Money mindset shifts and affirmations to help you anchor into more confidence, power, and abundance to elevate your business success
- Structures, systems, and support to help you scale your heart-centered business
- Practical needle-mover action steps to help you elevate into entrepreneurship
- Business and technical support recommendations to scale with ease

Learn more and claim your free BONUS Trainings + Workbook Bundle by opening the camera app on your cell phone and holding your phone over the QR code below like you're going to take a picture. The app will automatically pick up on the code and offer to take you to the correct webpage where you can claim the workbook by entering your name and email.

~~~

Always remember this—

You are a Queen.

A heart-centered lightworker. A healer.

A powerful channel for healing.

A beacon of light for all you serve.

Your business is the vehicle through which more love enters the world.

You were born for this.

~~~

Moving Beyond the Counter

FOREWORD

By Todd Eury

Owner of The Pharmacy Podcast Network, @pharmacypodcast

Foreword /ˈfôrˌwərd/

noun

1. A short introduction to a book, typically by a person other than the author.

So, there you have it. The evidence you were searching for to ensure the time you're about to invest reading this book will be *well* worth it.

Trust me, it will be.

This book will take you through a journey into yourself to become a heart-centered entrepreneur. To unlock and amplify your gifts to expand and elevate into entrepreneurship!

You as a provider are so talented and gifted. I know because I work with pharmacists every day at The Pharmacy Podcast™ Network. We have 130k listeners each month, with six episodes per week generated from 40+ contributors. I'm blown away that the Healthcare and IT Marketing Community voted Pharmacy Podcast the #1 Healthcare podcast in 2022.

We at The Pharmacy Podcast Network deliver excellent and reliable information, based on your evidence-based beliefs as Providers. You back your decisions based on evidence, and that practice saves lives. I live by these principles as a dedicated servant to the pharmacy profession to deliver evidence-based audio discussions in healthcare. I am amplifying pharmacists' voices through podcasting. I'm pretty good at what I do, but I can do more. I will do more.

But I had to learn this.

Take me back 18 years ago, and I knew nothing. I didn't know anything about pharmacy when I entered the profession in 2004. I knew nothing about pharmacists, except "they stand behind a counter and count pills."

I sold software to institutional pharmacies. I helped that company become a leader in Long Term Care (LTC) pharmacy software. They created the first Structured Query Language (SQL) database-driven software for LTC pharmacies. At that time, I realized that pharmacist success stories weren't being shared. There was nothing in audio form to help pharmacists learn from one other.

I can vividly remember driving in my car, listening to NPR, and thinking, *"Nothing covers our pharmacy profession or healthcare providers' modern healthcare."* I wasn't hearing the voices of the people I wanted to serve—pharmacists.

2009 —time to build a podcast about the profession to amplify the voices of pharmacists.

Decision. Boom. Launched, hasn't stopped since the beginning. Documenting pharmacists through audio is my gig. I love it. Podcasting is fun. Hard. But fun. The podcast became my work of art—tweaking it, refining it, and evolving it over time. It became the first network of podcasters dedicated to the profession of pharmacy.

I had to learn evidence-based principles that you learn in pharmacy school so that I knew I was delivering the best, most accurate information through this podcast.

This nation is hurting. In the past two years, we've moved through major issues like systemic racism, cancel culture, a major pandemic, and more. These events have led to division, but we need to come together as practitioners to bring more heart to how we serve.

Many pharmacists are burnt out. I want you to know that if you are experiencing burnout, it's not a weakness. It is part of a cycle to birth something brand new. We know what fire does to crops and to nutrients in soil—it destroys them so they can be built back up. There are nutrients in that fire-kissed soil that make it fertile ground for new growth.

Before I started The Pharmacy Podcast, I was burnt out from selling pharmacy software. I was good at it, but I was still burnt out.

Then after the burnout, I grew. Inside. (Probably outside too. I needed to lose about 14, maybe 17 ... call it 20ish pounds. Okay, 25. Geez.)

What I've done for you, you can do for others, and again, and again, and on, and on. I'm helping you help change our industry from the inside out. Through you!!

It took me years to finally push past the lack of confidence I had in myself. My belief in what pharmacists do every day was the impetus.

I had to learn to love myself first to help truly empower you with my full potential. I'm only 50% done. I had to believe I AM THE LEADER in podcasting for the advancement of the profession.

That's a Provider. You're a Provider regardless of what CMS (Centers for Medicare and Medicaid Services) defines you as.

And I'm so proud of you. Imagine what we will do #TogetheRx?

Dr. Christina Fontana taught me about my internal barriers and programming that I absorbed from my father. I was taught to always deliver value through hard work. I developed an internal story that I was only worthy if I worked hard. This became very cyclical in that it felt like a drug to get validation from the next contract, the next sale, the next win. I was only worthy if I was winning.

I realized how much I was limiting myself because of the programming I received as a child.

I absorbed beliefs from my dad, who didn't have enough confidence in himself. He didn't believe in himself enough to take the entrepreneur route. He took the safe route; a sure bet and stable career in the electrical industry.

He walked away from a multimillion dollar real estate career blossoming in the late 1970s in Orlando. He never reached for more, even though he was the #1 Rookie of the Year in Real Estate in Florida.

He walked. He quit. He went back to his trusted trade. He became a journeyman, and damn, he was the absolute best electrician reporting to some very powerful people and is still known today in the electrical business. I'm proud of my dad. I wanted to be the best just like him, but I was limited because that's what I saw modeled to me.

I also lacked the confidence. I had no proof or evidence to show that I was capable of greatness.

Christina and her dad have a similar story to my own. The Tarantolas were the best at what they did, building a valuable community pharmacy in Long Island. So, why walk away from the best thing that her dad built?

Because Christina knew there was more. She knew she was meant to take it "all the way up"— and she did. She just did. But she had to tune in to herself, take what her father taught her, and release what no longer worked.

So imagine what *you're* actually capable of doing without limits or holding onto old beliefs that are controlling you. You are LIMITLESS! The path of entrepreneurship requires vision, commitment, consistency, hard work, and belief in yourself. When you walk out in faith in yourself (and you may not see the evidence at first), so much is waiting for you on the other side.

Fulfillment.

Freedom.

Financial success.

Impact.

I want to amplify your voice because *you* are the future of heart-centered leadership in pharmacy.

Pharmacist, I'll leave you with this. Don't limit yourself based on your lack of confidence in yourself or let old beliefs hold you back or stop you. Make your decision, and move forward. The confidence comes. Believe me. I'm the first PodD in healthcare. (BTW, who do I call to get this accredited? DM me.)

Take this time to grow.

God bless you, my favorite Providers.

Christina, writing the foreword in your book is something I will never forget. Thank you, my friend.

Moving Beyond the Counter

INTRODUCTION

I know and trust that you've arrived here because you are ready for more fulfillment in your career as a health care practitioner. You're here to unlock and monetize your gifts to expand and elevate into entrepreneurship. And you know that you're meant for more.

You were drawn to the healing professions (like pharmacy, nursing, or medicine) because you want to help people get better and to make an impact in the world. You're a caring, nurturing person with a big heart, and you want to help your patients get healthier.

In pharmacy school, you were told that there were very few paths after graduation—retail, hospital, residency, or industry. Those were the paths you could take to use your degree and knowledge in the world.

You were taught to be professional, follow the rules and guidelines, and be conservative. That left very little room for creativity, self-expression, and voicing your needs and desires.

You may have been told (or believed) that you were "too much" or "not enough." That you had to tamp yourself down to "fit in" and be "good."

You graduated school excited to start working, but quickly got disillusioned by the reality of the broken healthcare system, feeling under-appreciated at your job, and the high demand of being a healthcare worker.

By the way, when I talk about "healthcare," one word, I'm referring to the system that we as pharmacists have traditionally worked in. But "health care," two words, is the overall care for one's health, which allows us the broader ability to care for the whole person, a modern, heart-centered approach.

If you are a woman of color, you may have experienced macro- and microaggressions, feeling misjudged and unwelcome in your own job, adding tremendous stress to an already demanding workload. You may have felt like you had to suppress your feelings about this, and as the years went by, you fell silent to these parts of yourself. The parts of *you* that make you, you.

Your inner light got snuffed out.

And the authentic, vibrant, radiant *you* slowly slipped away.

With the primary focus on script counts, number of vaccines given, long hours standing behind a counter without proper breaks, and the overwhelm of having to do it all perfectly—you're left feeling jaded, exhausted, and disheartened. Instead of feeling excited and fulfilled by your job, you're feeling burnt out, sacrificing your own health to help others be healthy.

If you're like me, you have a deep desire to truly make an impact on your patients and have the freedom and flexibility to do it on *your* terms. Somehow, that reality can feel so far away. Maybe you're overwhelmed, scrolling on your social media feed, unsure of where to start. Or you're feeling stuck because you don't know what course, program, certification, or action step to take. Trust me, I get it. Because I was there back in 2019.

At the time, I was working for a corporate retail chain pharmacy, working back-to-back 12-hour shifts without any proper breaks, feeling enslaved by the counter (and the job) that I so desperately wanted to come out from. I started having debilitating neck pain from looking down verifying orders all day and pinching the phone with my shoulder so my hands were free. I had to wear Thermacare patches every day to work to alleviate the pain even though I sought chiropractic care.

With the overwhelming task list, lack of breaks or fresh air, and minimal staffing support, I started having panic attacks on a weekly basis. I started Zoloft within six months of starting my job. I'd always worked in independent pharmacies before that, but this was a different beast.

The worst part of it all was feeling enslaved by these "golden handcuffs" that paid my bills, but deep down not knowing how to transition to full-time entrepreneurship. I'd been running my business since 2012, but stubbornly refused to hire a business coach. The fear was too intense because I had no safety net or guarantee that I could make my business work. So, I silently stuffed down my dreams, needs, and desires in exchange for a paycheck. I was miserable every day.

The front-store drama started to negatively impact my work as I was surrounded by constant complaining and bickering, which ultimately turned its ugly head toward me. The pressure got to be too much with all of the drama from the front-end, the never-ending task list, and trying to fill every prescription perfectly. After a particularly rough day in early April of 2019, I decided to quit retail for good. I called my district manager the next day, put in my two weeks, and never looked back.

Since then, I've built a multiple six figure per year business helping healers in health care unlock and monetize their gifts and own their brilliance to scale their profitable healing business. I'm utilizing my innate soul gifts of intuition, compassion, and empathy, along with the knowledge I've accrued over the last decade to help pharmacists move from *stuck* to *scaling* a profitable, heart-centered business.

I'm here to show you that creating a fulfilling career in health care is not only possible; it's here for you *now*. It's the reason I'm writing this book—to show you there is a better way for you to use your gifts and get paid abundantly for them. *(Insert sigh of relief.)*

If you're drawn to this book, you're most likely an out-of-the-box, non-traditional thinker. *That's a GOOD thing, by the way.* It takes tremendous courage to step out into entrepreneurship, owning all of who you are.

You also see and feel things on a deeper level and have a servant heart to help your patients HEAL rather than adding another medication onto their laundry list of prescriptions.

Of course, there is a time and a place for Western medicine, but you really want to help people heal through holistic means. You really want to move from healthcare worker to heart-centered healer, owning your gifts and getting paid abundantly for them.

Maybe you've seen healthcare entrepreneurs sprouting up all over the place in your Instagram feed, and you're drawn to being your own boss. You just may not know where to start.

I understand completely. We weren't taught how to launch and scale profitable businesses in pharmacy school. Over the last 10 years of being an entrepreneur, I've invested close to $300,000 in my own personal growth and business to adapt the principles I'll be teaching you in this book so your path is much easier and smoother as you transition out of your healthcare job into full-time, heart-centered entrepreneur.

Right now you might be feeling...

Stuck because you don't know "how" to grow a profitable business without sacrificing your family's income or leaving the safety and security of a stable paycheck.

Frustrated because you've been trying to figure this entrepreneur journey out on your own, but keep swirling in self-doubt and self-sabotage.

Anxious and overwhelmed with the coaches, certifications, and programs inundating you in your social media newsfeed.

And much more.

I get it. I'm here *with* you, Queen.

I am here to show you how to elevate from *burnt out* healthcare worker to *lit up* heart-centered entrepreneur so you can experience true fulfillment and freedom, while serving using your gifts and getting paid abundantly for them.

What you *may not* know is that you've been guided here to unlock and monetize your gifts, make a bigger impact, and enrich the world with *your* medicine. The medicine that can only come from your heart—compassion, love, and support that your clients really need. Yes, there is a place for medical intervention, but what I've learned over the past decade is that your clients really want to be seen, heard, and understood as they are moving through their transformation journey.

When a person feels deeply seen, heard, and understood, they feel safe to open up to talk about their diagnosis, medical condition, and healing journey.

You're *really* here to be ALL of you—fully self-expressed, unleashed, and unlocked. To do that, you have to release the blocks holding you back (feeling like a fraud, procrastination, perfectionism, etc.) so you can confidently step into your power, own your brilliance, and unlock your gifts to scale your profitable heart-centered business.

I always say that starting a business is easy, but growing a PROFITABLE business takes some deeper dive, inner transformation work.

For the first portion of the book, I'll be teaching you the timeless success principles I teach my clients in my Step into Your Queen: Elevate Entrepreneur Academy™, my signature program for heart-centered healers in health care to help you call in consistent clients and cash to scale your heart-centered business. I'll be showing you the smoother, simpler path to scale and how I went from homeless to creating a multiple six-figure per year business helping healers in health care create profitable heart-centered businesses.

In the second half of the book, you'll hear the stories of 19 brilliant pharmacist entrepreneurs who have monetized their gifts and have created successful heart-centered businesses. These women are seasoned heart-centered entrepreneurs who want to connect with you, so I encourage you to reach out to them.

You'll read the stories of these 19 incredible women who come from different backgrounds, ethnicities, cultures, and experiences. You'll see yourself in all of them, and I guarantee you'll be inspired that you *can* do this too.

You'll learn from women who have grown profitable businesses in the following areas:

- Functional Medicine
- Pharmacogenomics/Personalized Medicine
- Health + Wellness – Lifestyle Coaching, Weight Loss Coaching
- Holistic Health – Holistic Oncology, Herbalism
- Financial Coaching
- Women's Empowerment
- Fertility and Pregnancy
- Spiritual Life Coaching
- Stress Management

When you're moving through your transformation journey, you need support, and there is nothing like connecting with someone who's been there, done that, and wants to see you shine!

When you come from an open, abundant perspective in business, there is nothing you can't achieve. As you elevate into this higher perspective, you'll see that instead of competition, you'll form collaborations. Instead of coming from fear, you'll find connections. Every single woman in this book is ready to embrace you to walk with you.

It's allowed to be EASY and it's YOUR time to SHINE, Queen!

AWAKENING AND UNLOCKING YOUR INNER HEART-CENTERED HEALER

You don't have to be perfect to be a healer or to have a profitable heart-centered business. (Re-read that one again.)

You also don't have to feel like you've got it all figured out to start making an impact in your business or getting paid clients.

You already have these "codes" inside of you waiting to be unlocked. The energetic codes of your soul blueprint waiting to be opened to bring forth this heart-centered healer within you. You were born for this, Queen. You've been preparing for this your entire life.

Throughout this book, I'm going to show you how to turn your gifts, life experiences, challenges, and rock bottom moments into *gold* to use in your business. To shine your brilliant light and be a clear channel to pour *love* into your clients and into the world.

Your wounds carry wisdom. Instead of seeing them as weaknesses or that you need to be "fixed" or perfect to help others heal, you can see your wounds as a portal of power, healing, and transformation.

When you can own and share your own healing and transformation story, you empower, uplift, and inspire every single person your story touches. Your power lies in awakening and owning all aspects of your journey so you can be the beacon of light for others to know it's safe for them to share, too.

This is how we create a domino effect of healing in a world where we so often feel disconnected from each other. With the advent of social media, for entrepreneurs, it often feels isolating to watch the highlight reels of others without being able to witness what's really going on behind the scenes.

Being able to transmute shame, guilt, or fear into hope and inspiration is one of the most powerful ways you can BE in the world as an entrepreneur. Your clients and patients want to see the real, unfiltered, raw version of you. Because *that* is who they'll connect to.

So what does it really mean to heal?

When you hear the word "healer," your mind may go to the word "cure," which then gives a warning to your mind to use a disclaimer. I know—we learned about this in pharmacy school.

First, let me distinguish the difference between *curing* and *supporting healing*. I am not suggesting that you will be *curing* your clients and patients of their ailments. I am not suggesting you claim that you can do that. I am also not saying that *you* are the one doing the healing. You are a facilitator of healing through your love, support, coaching, and guidance. You are supporting your patients' and clients' healing process by seeing them as a WHOLE person—looking at their physical health along with their mind, body, spirit.

To "heal" means to make whole and restore health.

To me, a healer has unique attributes—

1. You are a channel of light and love for the world.
2. You are heart-centered and have a servant heart to help alleviate the suffering of others.
3. You are a bridge for other's transformation and healing.
4. You are empathetic, intuitive, and naturally gifted at sensing what's underneath someone's words.
5. You are drawn to healing in general—whether that is healing through meditation, prayer, crystals, Reiki, energy work, healing touch, hypnosis, subconscious programming, herbs, or other any other means to bring the body back into balance.
6. You see and feel things on a deeper level because you're an empath and highly sensitive person.

As a healthcare professional, you are already familiar with the broken healthcare system and the mantra "a pill for every ill." Our Western medical model often seeks to put a Band-Aid on to mask symptoms rather than treat or heal. As an example, a patient presents with symptoms of depression and is given an antidepressant without looking into nutrition, movement, meditation, or other forms of alternative healing. That patient then stays on that antidepressant for years.

This old paradigm of treating symptoms versus looking at the root cause is quickly changing. Healthcare professionals (HCP) are waking up to the various methods of healing that we were not taught in school. With the birth of the Internet and social media, HCPs are breaking out of the old mold of medicine and bringing forth these complementary and alternative ways of patient-centered care.

Now more than ever, pharmacists and HCPs are becoming coaches, empowering their patients by utilizing skills like Motivational Interviewing (MI)—an evidence-based approach to behavior change—to bring about positive health outcomes.

The effectiveness of MI is well-documented. The process empowers patients to take charge of their health. Pharmacists are uniquely positioned to become coaches as we've been trained in MI, the stages of change, and how to help our patients adapt health-promoting behaviors. Health coaching has become a new opportunity in the realm of pharmacy.

A health coach is defined as one who uses evidence-based skillful conversation, clinical interventions, and strategies to actively and safely engage clients/patients in health behavior change. Health coaches are certified or credentialed to safely guide clients and patients who may have chronic conditions or those at moderate to high risk for chronic conditions.

As noted in a study on adherence in *Therapeutics and Clinical Risk Management*, the data indicates that overall 40% of patients do not adhere to doctors' prescription recommendations. In addition, 35% neglected to fully follow through on suggested physical therapy directives. When it came to physician recommended changes in lifestyle habits, non-adherence hit 70%.

(Martin 2005) Pharmacists can help bridge the gap between physician vernacular—medical jargon can be overwhelming to many patients—and actionable steps the patient can take to improve their health.

For some patients, a feeling of disempowerment can substantially impair their ability to implement lifestyle changes and to adhere to medical directives. Ongoing communication, patient education, and support are needed to achieve the desired results of drug therapy. Health coaching helps empower patients to take ownership of their health and well-being. Health coaches model key skills related to lifestyle change and personal growth, empowering their clients with a sense of individual mastery and personal accountability.

According to a recent article in *Global Advances in Health and Medicine,* chronic conditions are typically brought on by poor lifestyle decisions and are the primary cause of death and disability in the United States. In Dr. Joe Dispenza's book *Breaking the Habit of Being Yourself*, he states that "around 95% of all illnesses are related to lifestyle choices, chronic stress, and toxic factors in the environment" (Dispenza 2012).

This is not suggesting that genetic predisposition is not a significant health predictor, but it *does* mean that we possess a greater capacity to improve our health prognoses than we once thought. Studies have shown that we can positively alter our gene expression and improve the signals our cells are receiving through stress-reduction practices, nutrient and supplement therapies, exercise, improved sleep, or even therapy to improve resiliency or to reprogram our responses to stressors.

Epigenetics suggests that a change in environmental/lifestyle factors creates a change in gene *expression*. Cells are constantly interacting with their environment and changing their gene expression in response; problems arise when these gene functions become stuck "on" or "off."

The connection between chronic stress (and the corresponding hyper-arousal of the body's stress response) and negative health outcomes (i.e., unfavorable genetic expression) comes down to the mind-body connection: our thoughts and internal states produce corresponding physiological responses in the body. As Dispenza writes, stress-induced emotions cue the genetic "dysregulation" of cells in ways that create disease. By consciously creating a life and environment in which you experience healthy, manageable levels of stress and non-damaging emotions, you are not contributing to the damaging health outcomes correlated with chronic stress.

Because lifestyle-related disorders are the primary reason for poor health, every patient can benefit from health coaching. As pharmacist coaches, we are the advocates, guides, and support for our patients and clients.

To become empowered and effective heart-centered coaches, it is important for HCPs to do their own inner transformation and healing work to positively impact patient outcomes.

As a coach, you are a leader and an example for your patient or client. Often we have our own internal barriers, triggers, and perspectives that need to be relinquished so we can truly have effective coaching sessions. It becomes imperative that you move through your own inner resistance and healing so you can serve others with empathy as a heart-centered practitioner.

According to MI research, practitioner empathy is the most important factor in a patient's health. In MI, empathy is simply the demonstration of neutral curiosity for the patient's ideas and attitudes regarding all sides of the behavior change being proposed. In other words, "empathy" refers to the idea that you "get" the other person. You really understand their point of view about this proposed change, and you have the ability to communicate your empathy. When people feel understood, they are more likely to share their experiences with us. Empathetic listening minimizes resistance and has a major impact on a client's willingness and capacity to change.

According to *Behavior Therapy Journal*, in MI, empathy is defined as "a specifiable and learnable skill for understanding another's meaning through the use of reflective listening" (Lord 2015). Coaches who are more empathetic expedite client outcomes, such as increased treatment engagement and change talk preceding behavior change. High levels of empathy are associated with positive results across a broad range of different therapies.

Sample expressions of empathy can sound like—

- "I can see how difficult this is for you."
- "That must have been challenging for you."
- "I'm sorry you're moving through this."
- "What has this been like for you?"
- "What do you need right now?"
- "I can't imagine what you must be going through right now."
- "This must be really hard to talk about. Thank you for trusting and opening up to me."

There is other science through the HeartMath®□ Institute to support developing these heart-centered qualities as practitioners. Research at the HeartMath Institute shows that adding heart to our daily activities and connections produces measurable benefits to our own and others' well-being.

According to The HeartMath Institute, the heart's electrical field is about 60 times greater in amplitude than the electrical activity generated by the brain, and the magnetic field produced by the heart is 100 times greater than that of the brain. This field, measured in the form of an electrocardiogram (ECG), can be detected anywhere on the surface of the body.

The heart's magnetic field, which is the strongest rhythmic field produced by the body, extends in all directions into the space around us. The heart's magnetic field can be measured several feet away from the body using sensitive magnetometers.

According to Heart Math research, our thoughts, breathing patterns, exercise, feelings, and emotions impact our heart rate variability (HRV) that leads in incoherence and dysregulation of the nervous system. On the other hand, feeling positive emotions leads to coherence and ordered heart rhythm patterns, aligning with health. See images below.

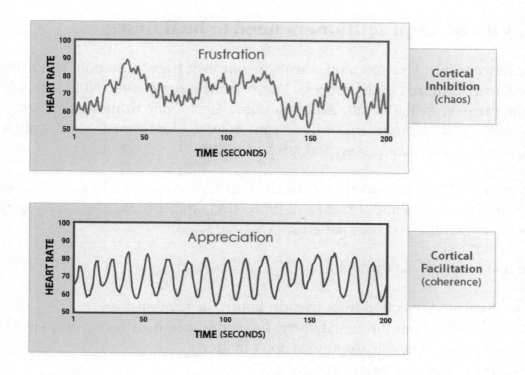

Source - https://www.heartmath.org/science/ (Chapter 06: Energetic Communication n.d.)

If we want to create true and lasting change in our world, we must start healing within our own hearts. True healing takes place within each person's heart as we awaken to the truth of who we are, which is healed, whole, and complete. As Ghandi said, "Be the change you wish to see in the world." We must remember that our patients are *people*, and a heart-centered approach to health care *is* the new paradigm.

To awaken and elevate your inner heart-centered healing ability means to move through your own inner healing/transformation journey to become aligned with your heart-centered, true Divine nature. It means that you journey within yourself into the parts of you that you may deny, avoid, suppress to face off with yourself and emerge more connected to your own heart. It means having the courage to feel the emotions that keep you looping in and out of vicious cycles to heal yourself first.

Why do we as practitioners need to heal first?

The short answer? As you move through your own transformation, you become more heart-centered in the process. You become more connected to love, which is the greatest healer of all. And you allow more *light* to move through you. Literally, you *lighten up* when you release resentment, self-criticism, judgments, guilt, shame, fear, and grief.

We've all had painful experiences in life that have caused us to subconsciously shut our hearts down as a means of protection, and this can negatively impact how we empathize with our patients.

You may have moved through...

- Repeated rejection from friends, family, or relationships
- Abandonment through divorce, break ups, death, or being left to feel that your feelings/voice/opinions don't matter
- Deep disappointment and pain
- Bullying, abuse, or mistreatment
- Racism, macro- or microaggressions, and discrimination
- Traumatic events
- Criticism and judgment from others because of the light you shine

Pain seeks protection.

When we subconsciously close down our hearts, we disconnect from ourselves and others. The more you shut down your heart, the more you become numb to your feelings, needs, and desires. On the other hand, the deeper you know yourself, the more deeply you can meet others.

Especially when starting a business as an entrepreneur, you may encounter many fears because you are stretching yourself out of your comfort zone in so many ways.

As some examples...

- You need to be able to clearly communicate your value to your audience and make offers for your programs or services. *This can bring up unworthiness, fear of being seen, or feeling overly responsible for the results you get your clients because they're paying you.*
- You will become more visible—being seen and heard on social media, your website, on podcasts, etc. *This brings up the fear of being seen or feeling like an imposter.*
- You'll be guiding your clients and creating offers, programs, social media copy, newsletter content, and more. *This brings up "analysis paralysis" (fear of making a wrong decision that keeps you from making a decision at all), perfectionism, procrastination, and the fear of not being good enough.*
- Instead of someone telling you what to do, you will be the one making the decisions on everything from your logo to your prices and beyond. *This can bring up fear of making a mistake, doing something wrong, or making the wrong choice.*

This comes up because, as pharmacists, we are conditioned to...

- Suppress our emotions, needs, desires, and opinions
- Put our heads down and work hard
- Override our bodily needs for food, bathroom breaks, or fresh air
- Not offer any input or suggestions or make requests
- Be "good" by not rocking the boat and doing what we were told

Fears of being seen, of failing, of succeeding, of shining, of not being good enough all come to the surface because of these past experiences and the way we were conditioned as HCPs.

Entrepreneurship is a totally new way of being and operating in the world. And it's very unfamiliar at first, which is why many pharmacists feel like imposters at the start.

For you to make the successful transition from healthcare worker to heart-centered full-time entrepreneur, you need both INNER transformation work AND practical strategy to scale.

One of the deepest subconscious fears of entrepreneurs (and human beings in general) is, "What if I open my heart and I show someone the light I shine and it's still not enough?" You naturally want to avoid feeling disappointment, rejection, criticism—which creates self-sabotaging behaviors that dim the light of your Divine true nature.

The amount of light that you shine is directly related to how deeply your heart is unconditionally open. To become a heart-centered healer in health care is to move through your own process of inner healing.

Healing comes from releasing and stripping away what is *not* love, so you can *become* love in action.

Releasing comes in many forms...

IDENTITY – Releasing shame and guilt from stories you've subconsciously created about who you are or what you've done.

FEARS – Releasing subconscious fears of shining your light and the negative consequences that come out of you being seen.

EXPECTATIONS – Releasing the weight of expectations from others—family, friends, etc.

JUDGMENTS – Releasing judgments and criticisms we have of ourselves and others.

FORGIVENESS – Forgiving yourself and others for past mistakes, behavior, conduct, and pain.

Healing through forgiveness does not mean that you condone bad behavior. It's about reclaiming your power through releasing the pain and forgiving yourself for ever thinking it was your fault or that you were the target of that person's pain. From the highest perspective, instead of holding onto the past and closing your heart down in painful protection, you can say, "Thank you for giving me the chance to open my heart."

As you move through this book, you'll have opportunities to move through the beginning stages of healing your heart to become a heart-centered healer.

When you release and let go, you "lighten up," allowing more light to shine through you and more love to radiate out into the world through the vessel of your business.

When you connect back to love, which is who you really are, your body naturally heals, you treat yourself and others with kindness, and your loving conduct is reflected in every action you take. You'll be able to meet your patients and clients with heart qualities—compassion, generosity, loving kindness, and equanimity. Your business will grow because you're operating from a higher frequency.

As a more tangible example to show the power of love on the human body, imagine you have two seeds and put them in separate planters. With seed #1, you rarely tend to it. You occasionally check in on it to give it water but most often it's getting minimal nourishment. You speak hateful words over it, asking why it isn't growing. With seed #2, you nurture it, giving it sunlight, water, and constant care. You say loving and kind things to it. Which seed will flourish? The same thing is happening within your own body and this idea was supported by a Japanese researcher, Dr. Masaru Emoto.

Emoto studied how our thoughts, words, and emotions impact our inner landscape. For over 20 years until he passed away in 2014, he studied the scientific evidence of how the molecular structure in water transforms when it is exposed to human words, thoughts, sounds and intentions. He used the medium of water to study how the molecules responded to various frequencies (anger, hate, love, etc.) He did this through magnetic resonance analysis technology and high-speed photographs. The following images show some of his findings.

When he spoke words of love and gratitude, the structure of water became organized and arranged in beautiful patterns. When he spoke words of hate, the structure of the water became erratic and unorganized. Love is our true Divine nature.

Eternal

Peace

Love and Gratitude

You Disgust Me

Evil

Thank You

Source - https://thewellnessenterprise.com/emoto/ (Dr. Masaru Emoto and Water Consciousness n.d.)

The same thing happens with our thoughts and emotions as we speak love over ourselves. What we say impacts our physical health and how we view ourselves and others in the world, including our clients and patients. Understanding more about being loving with ourselves will help us be loving with those we interact with. We must embody and BE love to GIVE love.

LOVE is a state of BEING that is unconditional. It doesn't give to receive. It doesn't waiver or withdraw love when someone cannot meet it or receive it. It just IS. But sometimes, we learn that love is conditional, which leads us to loving and then seeking reciprocity, feeling drained by the love we give.

When you're an empath—as most healers are—and you feel everything on a deep level, you love a lot more than other people. Because of this, to avoid feeling drained, you have to lean into the unconditional nature of love and learn to give without expecting reciprocity or expecting everyone to know how to receive it. And when you still choose to shine your light into the world for people who don't know how to receive it, your love will be a strength because you have learned to be unconditional with your giving. You open the way for others to love unconditionally as well because you are holding space for them to do so.

Deeper levels of mastery involve knowing that even in the face of others who push away your love or are unable to receive it, you ask yourself, "How much more can I open my heart?"

When you hold your love back, everything hurts. This is conditional love. It means you're judging who gets more or less of your love based upon their conduct or deservingness. You're often waiting for others to receive you (and give love to you) in a way that they can't even give to themselves. This is the fertile training ground for heart-centered mastery.

Opening your heart to shine your love, without being concerned with who will receive, judge, criticize, or push it away IS how we become anchors of light in this world. It's how we create Heaven on Earth, bringing forth well-being for all on this planet.

The word "vulnerability" comes from the Latin word, "wound." Being vulnerable means having the ability to go into your wounds. This inner healing journey is about having the courage to witness your wounds with compassion to heal, release, and *open your heart* to serve your clients with the most powerful medicine on the planet—LOVE.

This is how you become a heart-centered healer—a beacon of light in the world.

This is how we create a new paradigm for healing in health care.

THE NEW PARADIGM FOR HEALING IN HEALTH CARE

Deep and lasting healing and transformation involves so much more than a Band-Aid solution or a simple quick fix. Over the last 10 years of studying Western medicine, pharmaceuticals, Reiki, MI, applied kinesiology, quantum physics, Eden energy medicine, hypnosis and subconscious programming, and more, I've found several principles to be true about healing and scaling a profitable business.

Principle #1. The majority of disease starts in the energetic realm as recurring patterns, beliefs, and thoughts and eventually becomes physical illness.

This is supported by the results of recent epigenetic research conducted by Dr. Joe Dispenza among others.

Quantum physics demonstrates that 99.9999999% of everything in our world is made up of energy and 0.0000001% is physical. Thoughts and emotions are energy forms, and when woven through our body over and over again, they create patterns.

For example, if a child is emotionally, physically, or mentally abused repeatedly, she creates a story about herself. She has certain thoughts that create emotions (energy in motion) that result in an energetic pattern. Her nervous system moves into fight, flight, freeze, or fawn to remain safe. The more deeply woven the pattern, the more subconscious and automatic the behavior becomes. Because the body is the subconscious mind, she may hold trauma in a certain area of the body, resulting in dis-ease.

As the subconscious mind adapts to survive, different patterns develop as mechanisms for self-protection. As an example, the little girl learns to people please to gain affection and love. Or she learns to be perfect and get good grades in school to win her parents' attention and praise. She absorbs the silent perspective to be "seen and not heard" and learns to suppress her needs, desires, and voice. She has learned that love is given conditionally, if she is "good."

Because the entrepreneurship journey is so intimately connected to SELF, often it brings these patterns to the surface. These learned coping mechanisms trickle into how you serve your patients, especially as you grow a business. All of your deepest fears come up to be witnessed in this fertile ground of entrepreneurship.

Some of the most common fears I see in my transformational business coaching practice are:

- Fear of being seen and shining your light
- Fear of success—this sounds silly, but it's true!
- Fear of failure
- Fear of making the wrong decision (analysis paralysis and overthinking)
- Fear of making other people angry (codependency and people pleasing)
- Fear of not being perfect (perfectionism)
- Fear of being judged/criticized
- Fear of looking bad

When you are fettered with these fears, patterns, and subconscious coping mechanisms, your energy is drained by suppressing, avoiding, and denying this part of you.

We will dive deeper into this in the Overcoming Self-Sabotage chapter.

Principle #2. True healing occurs in the body; your body is your subconscious mind.

In many personal development teachings, we bypass the body through focusing on our mindset. While having a positive mindset can be helpful in short-term situations, it does not lead to true healing. Have you ever said positive affirmations that didn't feel true to you? The body is so wise that it knows it has not accepted it as truth yet.

Deeper healing modalities like subconscious work, somatic healing, hypnotherapy, and breathwork are needed to release old programming, beliefs, and patterns. "Mindsetting" your way through challenges is bypassing the very essence of where the trauma lies—in the body.

The body is the subconscious mind and keeps an emotional record of your past. Your aura and energy field carry around the memories, emotions, traumas, and beliefs you've been programmed with. Unresolved trauma often results in being disconnected from your body through dissociation, where you're literally cut off from feeling your feelings.

A trauma is any deeply disturbing or distressing experience and is personal to you. What may have felt like a trauma to you may have been a completely different experience to someone else in the room. When a trauma happens, there is a split between the actual emotion and the thought/memory. Your body is in shock and cannot properly digest the emotion because high frequency gamma waves shock the brain. This describes the phenomenon of having the faint memory of an experience, but not being able to access details.

As a tangible example, I want you to imagine that you've eaten a piece of pizza, but you have no mechanism to digest it. The pizza stays in your body and cannot be digested or eliminated. This is what happens with undigested traumas in the body—the energy of the emotion remains in the body without any means to exit.

The energy of the emotion has to move somewhere, so it will move either inward to punish self or outward to blame others. As one small example, if you have a core wound of unworthiness, you may self-sabotage by underpricing your offers or believing people won't buy what you have. Another way this unworthiness wound can be triggered is if a potential client says "No" to your offer, which may cause you to create stories about how you're not good enough.

This is why inner healing is so powerful and important as you grow a business. If you aren't addressing your core wounds, subconscious programming, and identity, it's going to be difficult to create a new reality for yourself. You'll often find you're looping in and out of vicious cycles of self-sabotage, staying stuck.

This leads into the third principle.

Principle #3. You are a powerful creator of your reality.

Your energy and frequency create your reality. If you're walking around with undigested core wounds, limiting beliefs, and disempowering subconscious programming, growing your business will feel like climbing a mountain with a heavy backpack.

When you own that you have subconsciously or consciously created everything in your life, you become empowered. Many people resist this idea at first, but I want to lovingly challenge you to see this from a higher perspective.

David Hawkins was a researcher who studied human consciousness over 20 years. He used applied kinesiology to muscle test individuals to see where they calibrated on the Scale of Consciousness that follows. He mapped out a logarithmic scale called Power vs. Force that showed various levels of human consciousness.

What he found was that anyone who calibrated under 200 hz (courage) demonstrated self-destructive behaviors like smoking, drinking, binging, addictions, etc. The people at these lower levels were disempowered in their health and life. They blamed other people for their life experience and were often victims to their circumstances.

When someone calibrated over 200, they had life-giving behaviors and took ownership over their life. They held beliefs that supported their autonomy and realized that they were the creators of their reality rather than a victim to it.

Hawkins's work shows that as you release, surrender, and let go of the lower levels of consciousness (shame, guilt, fear, apathy) you naturally rise to more empowered states. As you rise in power, you are able to impact more people around you just by your "being-ness." It is with this deep inner transformation work that we can rise to the higher levels of awareness to experience joy, love, acceptance, and willingness.

Enlightenment| 700+
Peace | 600
Joy |540
Love |500
Reason |400
Acceptance | 350
Willingness | 310
Neutrality |250
Courage | 200
Pride |175
Anger | 150
Desire |125
Fear | 100
Grief | 75
Apathy | 50
Guilt | 30
Shame | 20

Flow

Getting By

Suffering

Figure 1 David Hawkins's Scale of Consciousness (hz)[1]

Hawkins's research shows that as you calibrate into the higher levels of consciousness, your impact exponentially elevates. Someone who calibrates at the level of willingness (310) can counterbalance 90,000 people under 200. An individual who calibrates at the level of love (500) can counterbalance 750,000 people under 200. As I mentioned earlier, this is because it is a logarithmic scale, increasing by the power of 10 rather than numerically.

According to the Attractor Field Model discovered by Dr. Kurt Ebert, thoughts and intentions generate energetic fields that either have a positive or deleterious effect upon our physical body. Attractor fields are nonphysical energy fields generated by each individual's attitudes, beliefs, and ongoing thought stream. These energy fields interact not only with your body, but also with the energy fields and bodies of others as well. It is as a result of these energy fields that you view the world the way that you do, and those

[1] Rainbow gradient image courtesy of Sharon McCutcheon, https://unsplash.com/@sharonmccutcheon

fields are why you have the attitudes and reactions toward life that you do. Like a magnet, your aura (energetic body) holds these attractor fields and will often link up with similar attractor fields. *Like attracts like.*

Thoughts that have negative energetic effects include shame, guilt, anger, fear, and false pride. Behaviors include blaming, judging, hiding, punishing, attacking, and criticizing. Positive thoughts and behaviors include acceptance, openness, love, curiosity, compassion, and forgiveness. Although seemingly simple, these principles are the foundation of how applied kinesiology (muscle testing) works and how Hawkins was able to test his subjects. Energetically, a truthful statement will strengthen the body, while a false statement will weaken it.

If you notice, I do not say to fight against or resist the lower levels, but to surrender to them, loving the parts of you that want to judge yourself for having the experience or emotion. Loving something doesn't mean you accept or condone it. It means you are willing to feel it, observe it, and love yourself through it to release it.

Releasing techniques like forgiveness, tapping, somatic healing, meditation, and energetic cord cutting will all help elevate your own power as you become a heart-centered healer.

As you move through surrendering the lower layers of shame, guilt, fear, grief, and move up into the higher levels of awareness, you begin to move away from suffering and start experiencing more flow and synchronicity in your life. You become more connected to your heart and your own true Divine nature, able and open to serve your clients and patients with more power, ease, and flow.

As you move through your own journey, you have deeper levels of compassion for humankind and literally *become* a heart-centered healer. As you witness your past experiences from a renewed lens, you take your power back and can use the energy that was once blocked toward creation and life-giving endeavors.

This is the new paradigm for health care—to awaken your own inner healer to be the change to empower your patients.

This is how we create a domino effect of healing in the world. And it starts within your own heart.

Moving Beyond the Counter

My Journey of Healing through the Heart

During the summer that I turned 7, I had a lemonade stand. My childhood friend Gina and I sat outside at the end of my cement driveway with pitchers, cups, and an envelope for money. We charged $1.00 for a cup of iced tea or lemonade and replenished the stock with ice intermittently. We had our own system, and at the end of the day, we'd split the earnings, ride our bikes down to 7-Eleven, spend the earnings on Slurpees or candy, and save the rest.

This was my first encounter with entrepreneurship. And I loved it. I loved the immediate gratification of seeing my work leading to tangible results. My dad taught me from a young age to "work hard" to get results, so that belief was deeply ingrained. Little did I realize that working hard was also intimately tied to my self-worth and that the seed of those beliefs would impact me as an adult entrepreneur.

During that time, I can remember drawing pictures and hanging them all over the house with signs that read "5 cents." My parents paid me, too!

I would also pretend I was a waitress at the breakfast table and take orders for pancakes, eggs, bacon, and juice. I was a mini entrepreneur!

It was around that time that my father started taking me to work on Saturdays at his drug store, Winn Drugs, on the North Shore of Long Island. I swept the floors, helped grandparents find birthday cards for their grandkids, made "photostat" copies on the copy machine, and turned vitamin bottles so the labels faced out.

During those days at Winn Drugs, I keenly watched my father—how he interacted with customers (his tone, gesturing, and body movements). I gleaned so much simply by observing the way he assuaged customers who were upset or asked about each customer and their family members. I was amazed by how he could recall details and names of each customer and their family members. He was jocular, full of life, and such a natural conversationalist. It all seemed so effortless.

I was also completely terrified of my father. He was a strict Italian father with a short temper. From a young age, I was conditioned that working hard lead to success. I could not feel my feelings, and God forbid if I cried in public. I'd get punished immediately. I knew that if I got "the look" from my dad I was in deep trouble and a verbal or physical action would be taken.

I was both enthralled by his power and debilitated by it. Growing up, I just kept my mouth shut, did what I was told, and tried my best to be good to get love and affection.

When I graduated to being a cashier at the pharmacy, I modeled and honed the people skills and behaviors I'd learned from him. People typically opened up to me right away—sharing stories and personal challenges that I hadn't asked about. It was in those moments at the pharmacy that I felt this deep inner pull to help people for a living. I knew I wanted to be a pharmacist and be just like my dad, and nothing would stop me.

After multiple SAT tests (it took 4 times to hit that 1200 mark), I applied and was accepted into St. John's University for the PharmD program. I was devoted to getting my pharmacy degree and eagerly studied the entire way through school.

It wasn't until I was in my final year of pharmacy school that all of that changed. I began getting a deep desire to do something different. I'd always thought that after school I would work for my dad. But suddenly my seven-year-old entrepreneur reappeared, and I felt a strong pull to pursue a nontraditional path within pharmacy. I wasn't sure exactly what it would look like, but I knew I needed to do a residency to get there.

At the time, I was moving through a rare eating disorder called "night eating syndrome," where I would get up at least twice a night and binge on any unhealthy food I could get my hands on. I would restrict my food during the day, and then eat uncontrollably at night. This nightly vicious cycle left me riddled with guilt every morning, yet I couldn't seem to stop.

On top of the eating disorder, my parents weren't happy with my decision to break out of the family business and do something nontraditional. I believe my father wanted me to take over the independent pharmacy, but it wasn't in my heart.

When I told my parents I wanted to do a residency, they were furious, and my dad could barely look at me. My parents thought I was betraying the family by choosing this other path. Nothing I said could convince them that this wasn't a decision meant to slight them, but to further expand my experience and gifts as a pharmacist.

I can clearly remember my mother standing in our kitchen, filled with anger shouting at me, throwing a plastic mustard bottle toward me and barely missing. She couldn't understand my wishes either, and deep down, I knew I was being punished for my innate desires. I'd never spoken up to my parents and had always been a "good girl"—a straight "A" student, top 10 in my high school class, captain of the kickline team. I stayed in the lines, and I was about to color way outside of them.

Despite the verbal bashing I received, I didn't care. I knew in the deepest part of me that I was meant to do something GREAT in the world—something big. I had no idea what it was, but I knew I was about to embark on the journey of the start of my new life.

I thought the abuse at home was the worst it would get, but I was terribly wrong.

Winn Drugs was the only place I'd ever worked, and I had never been on an interview before, let alone had a resume. I worked hard for a year getting all of those things in line, buying business cards, getting help with my resume, and practicing interviewing skills at St. John's University with professors and classmates.

It wasn't until I actually got the residency that I hit my rock bottom moment. I was at work when I got the call from the residency director at Kings Pharmacy in Brooklyn congratulating me that I was chosen for the position. Both elated and terrified, I went in the back room to my dad's office and told him. He was staring at the ceiling when I walked in and responded calmly with a deflated "congratulations."

That night, I had to go over my friend's house to study for an exam and a barrage of angry text messages funneled through my iPhone. My mom was furious that I got the residency and was due to move out of the house that June. My nerves were shot, and I felt that the only way out of the immense guilt I felt was to get drunk. My friend and I went to a bar in Massapequa, and I passed out on her couch that night.

The next day I got a text from my mom saying, *"You better come get all of your stuff. It's out on the lawn."* It felt like I had a heartbeat in my head, but I knew I had to rush back to my house before all of my belongings were thrown into the trash.

I arrived at the house to find my mother hysterically flinging my belongings out. She took coats and clothes with the hangers still attached and flung them onto our wooden porch. She blocked the entry to the house and said I wasn't allowed back inside.

I had around $4,000 in cash that I had been saving, and I wasn't allowed access to that either. My dad walked up to me in the driveway, demanding I give back the drug store key, and I knew I was fired.

I felt completely powerless, but in that moment something deep inside told me that I was on the cusp of a huge breakthrough and that my life would never be the same again.

There's something so powerful and thrilling about not having anything else to lose because everything you once knew has been stripped away. That day in April 2012, I lost my job, my family, my home, and any semblance of a normal life. I had nothing but the clothes on my back and all of my belongings stuffed into my tiny Mazda 3 sedan.

I was 23 at the time about to graduate pharmacy school, take my remaining two pharmacy board exams, and start my residency that June.

It was exhilarating to finally feel free, but it was also terrifying. The day after I got kicked out, I got a job, started looking for apartments, and began studying for my exams. I was determined to succeed and didn't have much time to integrate or process what had transpired the day before.

Luckily, I had a friend to stay with as I looked for an apartment, and I wound up passing my exams and graduating pharmacy school.

Little did I realize that my entire life had been preparing for that moment. I'd had the training from my dad to be independent, and this was my chance to make it on my own.

Going from experiencing a traumatic event right into a residency was no easy feat. I experienced weekly meltdowns, and my body was under tremendous stress.

During my pharmacy residency, I decided to pursue my passion for nutrition and signed up to become a health coach through the Institute for Integrative Nutrition coaching program. I was moving through my own healing journey and wanted to better help my diabetes patients at the pharmacy.

My residency director, Dr. Chawla, and I shared a small office in the back of the independent pharmacy. We wound up having many deep conversations about the trauma I'd experienced getting kicked out of my house, spirituality, life coaching, nutrition, healing, and so much more. She was also going through a spiritual awakening at the time, and I know now that our connection was a Divine appointment.

She was my first unofficial "coach" and stretched me out of my comfort zone, challenging me to dive into different books, teachings, and ways of thinking. As I was moving through Integrative Nutrition, she started life coaching school.

We supported each other's growth even though we were 10 years apart in age and she was my director. She even helped me enroll my first health coaching client from the cohort of diabetes patients we had at the pharmacy.

It was a special relationship and I grew so much because of those conversations and "sessions" with her in our office.

For the next several years after the residency, I voraciously devoured content from other coaches and healers. I started selling Young Living essential oils, listening to healers like Caroline Myss, Wayne Dyer, Louise Hay, Christine Hassler, Gabrielle Bernstein, and more.

I lived in a small studio apartment in Howard Beach, Queens at the time—working full time at another independent pharmacy, taking online classes with Integrative Nutrition, and focusing on my own healing.

Any extra money I made went into investing in my business. I immersed myself in deep dive transformational experiences with other entrepreneurs in conferences like Tony Robbin's Unleash the Power Within and programs like Landmark Worldwide. I was hungry for knowledge, healing, and transformation. I intuitively knew how much power was on the other side of my healing.

At the time, I was estranged from my parents and siblings and felt so alone in those quiet moments in the apartment at night. The weekly roller coaster of emotions, guilt, shame, and fear coursed through my body, and I needed a lot of support to heal from the trauma I'd experienced.

My eating was so out of control, so I started seeing an eating disorder specialist named Judy Stein at that time, too. Judy taught me about cognitive distortions (black-and-white thinking, catastrophizing, mind reading) and how to quiet my mind through meditation and loving kindness practices.

One night while I was meditating on my beige living room couch, I vividly remember fighting with my ego, so desperately wanting to go do something to keep "busy" instead of be with myself. My mind raced a lot, and it was so tough to sit still with all of the pain I was holding in my body.

I forced myself to just sit still and BE, and gradually the grip of my ego fell away. My mind was suddenly clear and at peace. It was during that meditation session that I saw an image of myself on a big stage with a microphone speaking. It was so REAL to me, and I heard the words, "This is what you're meant for." In that small studio apartment that night, I began to get glimpses of my purpose. God showed me what my destiny was, and even though I had no tangible proof, I trusted it.

Little synchronicities started happening after that. I'd hear about a book I had to read or a teacher I should listen to, and the message from the content was exactly what I needed at the right time. The more I meditated, the clearer my path became, and I just followed the guidance.

Along my healing journey, I became fascinated with topics I'd never learned in pharmacy school—epigenetics, quantum physics, Reiki, hypnotherapy, applied kinesiology, subconscious programming, somatic healing, and more. The more I learned, the more the root of my physical illness (eating disorder, anxiety, depression) finally revealed itself.

It was a long road to recovery as I unwound decades of abuse and limiting beliefs and stories about who I was.

Fast forward to 2019. I had healed myself of my eating disorder and started coaching women on their transformation journeys. I was still working in retail pharmacy at the time, but my heart was elsewhere. In my heart, I knew I was a facilitator of healing for women and that there was another layer of embodiment I hadn't quite owned yet.

At the time, I was too scared to invest in myself to hire a coach, but I knew I needed help to leave my career in pharmacy and become a full-time entrepreneur. I prayed that God would give me a sign and that I'd follow if He made it clear to me.

A few days later, a local coach in Pittsburgh sent an email with the subject line, "She said no to a six-figure job." The email went on to mention how this coach had helped her client earn consistent $10k months in her business. I immediately messaged the coach and asked how I could do the same. I invested close to $20,000 in that coach, quit my job, and never looked back. I went to work implementing what she suggested and made my investment back in 2 months.

Everything was going well, but then I hit a plateau. I was getting on calls with potential clients and they all said some version of "No." "No, I don't have the time." "No, I don't have the money." It was a consistent, frustrating pattern I saw that left me feeling helpless and discouraged. Despite the strategies my coach had given me, I felt stuck and feared having to go back to retail pharmacy.

Around that time, I started following a transformation coach and felt a strong pull to go to her 3-day retreat in San Diego. The investment for the three-day retreat was $6,000 and I was challenged again to invest in myself because I had very little money coming in. I followed my desire and told myself, "I love myself. I trust myself." Whenever I am investing in myself and there is any doubt or fear, I say that mantra, and it helps me anchor into faith, knowing I'm always supported.

The three-day retreat was so transformative for me, helping me unravel some of my deepest wounds such as unworthiness, control, perfectionism, and rigidity that were keeping me in lower frequencies. Right after that retreat, I made $18,000 in one week and filled my Quantum Queen program. My energy had opened up as I released the shame, guilt, fear, anger, and low-frequency patterns. I knew I was onto something, and as I began to implement similar techniques with my clients, they saw the same results.

As I was taken into the depths of my own healing journey, I uncovered the true needle mover to create an impact through entrepreneurship—inner transformation work. I started to notice that my pharmacist clients also had similar patterns to what I had gone through.

The repeated patterns in my pharmacist clients seemed to be universal—perfectionism, unworthiness, people pleasing, fear of shining, overthinking, and control issues. These patterns were learned survival mechanisms that had served them at some time in their life, but were keeping them small, safe, and unable to receive higher levels of income for their programs, sessions, and offerings. The energy from the emotional patterns became stuck in their bodies in different chakra centers, causing them to subconsciously close their hearts down in fear, leading to "blocks" to receiving.

"Chakra" is a Sanskrit word that means "wheel" or "vortex" referring to how the energy flows in key points in the human body. There are seven major chakras located along the spine. Each one of them vibrates at a different speed and each one emits a specific color with all of them together forming a beautiful color spectrum.

The chakras generally spin clockwise. As they spin, they bring energy from photons, the light particles in the universe and space around us, into the body to support and improve how our organs and systems are functioning along with the oxygen that we breathe and the nutrients we eat. On a physical level, a chakra's location dictates which area of the body it is responsible for the wellbeing of.

When the chakras are functioning properly—that is when they're open and cleared—we feel energized, more alive, and happier. We are at peace with where we are in our lives and clear on how we are moving forward to greater fulfillment.

In contrast, the moment we start stressing and worrying about things in our lives, our energy centers close down. When the chakras are blocked due to stress, lack of sleep, improper diet, lack of exercise, among other stressors, our body is not getting the energy it needs to function at its best, so we experience depletion. That's why it so important to maintain a practice of catering to the wellbeing of your body and your chakras.

Events in our lives and the way we react to them can cause our energy to get stuck, much like my clients see from the patterns from learned survival mechanisms I mentioned earlier. The places in our body where the energy gets stuck are the energy centers associated with the issues you're dealing with.

If, for example, a person has been sexually abused or has been conditioned since childhood to think that sex is bad, their energy can stay stuck in the first center, near the base of the spine, associated with sexuality, and they may have problems accessing creativity. If a person doesn't necessarily feel safe enough to use their creativity in the world, or if they have been traumatized or betrayed by another person, they might hold on to that energy in their second center, just below the navel. Such a person would be likely to feel excessive amounts of guilt, shame, suffering, low self-esteem, or fear.

If a person can get their energy flowing up to the third center, a few inches above the navel, but they have ego issues and they feel self-important, self-absorbed, controlling, domineering, angry, overly competitive, and bitter, then their energy gets stuck in their third center. They may have control issues or motivation issues. If a person cannot open their heart and feel love/trust or if they are afraid to express love or how they truthfully feel, energy can also become frozen in the fourth and fifth centers, respectively—located near the heart and in the throat.

The first three centers are where energy tends to get stuck most often. When it's stuck, it cannot flow into the higher energy centers between the eyes and at the crown of the head, where we're in love with life and want to give back.

What I've found is that a block is anywhere we have shut down and stopped love within ourselves. The journey of inner healing involves a multi-faceted approach through guidance of a coach who can facilitate transformation using specific healing/transformation tools.

Some examples of transformation tools are—

- Inner child healing
- Cord cutting
- Forgiveness work
- Self-love and self-care practices
- Emotional release techniques
- Subconscious clearing
- Breathwork
- Power reclamation exercises
- Sound healing frequencies
- And more

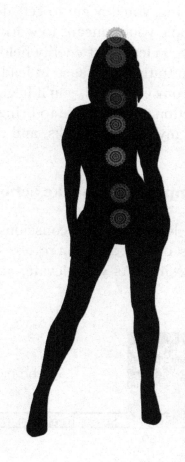

Figure 2 The Chakras

When you move through this releasing work, several things start to happen—

#1. You shift your reality because you're elevating your energy.

When you shift your internal energy, you'll see your external reality change. You may see friends or family exit your life because you no longer resonate with them. You may see shifts in your behaviors and habits, resulting in more natural, healthy choices.

#2. You'll experience more synchronicities to lead you along your path.

Because your vibration is rising, you'll begin to get "downloads" of action steps you're supposed to take, people you're meant to work with, or books/resources you're meant to absorb. As you clear your energy field of density, you're able to hear, see, feel, and receive intuitive messages to lead you on the next steps of your journey. As you quiet your ego mind, you'll begin to hear inner nudges of your true desires and the action steps to take to bring that desire into fruition. This is how I channel all of my content, books, and action steps that I take in my business.

#3. You become more empowered to take action.

In the following image, the lower levels of consciousness result in stagnation and inaction. The energy is denser and you're less motivated to take action toward your dreams and desires. As you elevate, you experience more flow, ease, and synchronicity.

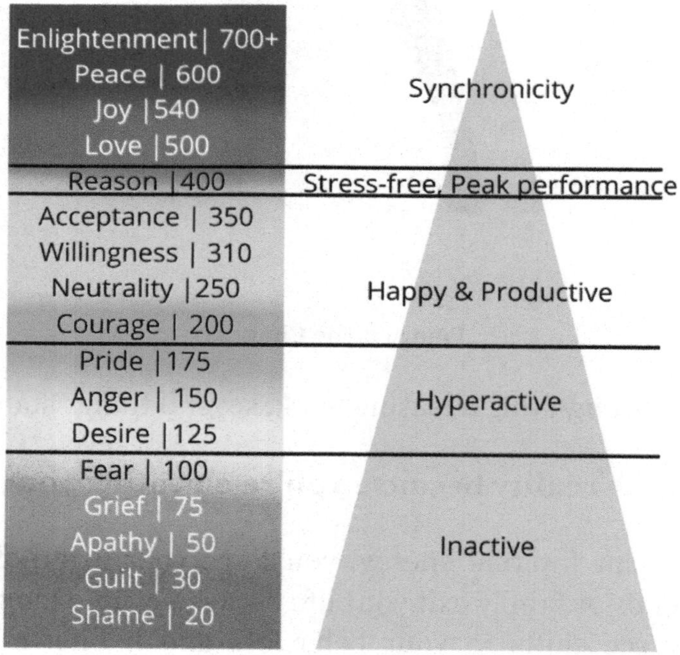

Figure 3 Scale of Consciousness Compared to Performance

Up until this point, you've read about the concepts and science of transformation, healing, releasing, and raising your consciousness to become more heart-centered.

In the next part of this book, I'll be sharing how to *Step into Your Queen to Scale Your Heart-Centered Business* through these 5 steps:

Step #1. Unlock Your Rare and Regal Soul Gifts + Becoming the Queen of Your Business

Step #2. Overcome Self-Sabotage to Feel Safe to Shine

Step #3. Release Money Memories to Receive Abundantly for Your Gifts

Step #4. Communicating, and Delivering Your Brilliance to Call in Your Soul Clients

Step #5. Create Systems, Structure, and Support to Scale Your Profitable Business

You'll find more in-depth trainings and an accompanying workbook in the Step into Your Queen: Scaling Your Heart-Centered Business BONUS Bundle.

Now let's dive into your transformation journey to help activate your heart-centered healer to scale your profitable business!

STEP #1. UNLOCKING YOUR RARE AND REGAL SOUL GIFTS + BECOMING THE QUEEN OF YOUR BUSINESS

The entrepreneurial journey often starts way before you create your LLC, business name, or start putting your content online. You've been preparing for this your entire life. Your brilliance—your rich and rare soul gifts, life experiences and lessons, and healing abilities—is already within you. Now it's about unlocking and owning those gifts to create a profitable business.

This is exactly how I help my pharmacist entrepreneur clients, so you're reading the right book!

When you're starting and scaling a business, many questions are running through your mind.

You're asking yourself...

- *Who is my ideal client? What is my niche?*
- *Where do I start?*
- *What certifications, programs, or coaches should I invest in?*
- *How much should I charge for my services?*
- *Where do I find clients?*
- *How do I put myself out there?*
- *How will I be able to run my business? I'm so busy!*
- And many more questions!

Here's what I'll tell you.

Running your own business requires a new way of thinking and being that is way different than working in a pharmacy or at a traditional healthcare job. Collectively, we are taught from a young age that we have to work really hard to achieve results. Working 12-hour shifts back-to-back without breaks and pushing through to get as many prescriptions done perfectly is the norm in retail pharmacy. Most of us were not taught to honor our voice, desires, and needs and to prioritize ourselves. As you can see, that model has not worked in healthcare.

According to *U.S. Pharmacist Magazine*, recent survey results reveal that 61.2% of pharmacists report experiencing a high level of burnout in practice, which is one of the highest rates among healthcare professionals. This rate is higher than that found in surgeons, oncologists, and emergency-medicine practitioners. (Elizabeth H. Padgett 2020)

When I graduated from pharmacy school back in 2012, there were limited options—retail, hospital, specialty pharmacy, residency, or going into industry. I never dreamed that I could have my own profitable online business. It simply wasn't an option that was discussed or seemed available at the time.

All of that is changing now. It's my mission to empower other pharmacists to see what's possible, which is one of the main reasons for this book.

The disempowered masculine programming we've been conditioned to follow told us that working hard led to results. We all have masculine and feminine energies within us. The tables below show the disempowered and empowered masculine energy along with the disempowered and empowered feminine energy.

Disempowered Masculine Qualities	Empowered Masculine Qualities
Forcing, pushing, controlling, striving to achieve outcomes	Self-led action based upon feminine desire
Controlling through overthinking and overanalyzing to "get" clients	Grounded and present with clients, while trusting yourself

No clear structure to funnel clients into your offers	Clear calls to action to lead clients into your offers
Rigid, guarded boundaries and avoiding asking for help	Having structures, systems, and support in place

Disempowered Feminine Qualities	Empowered Feminine Qualities
Emotions are suppressed and feeling/emoting is seen as "weak"	Allowing emotions to flow and to feel safe in expressing all parts of you
People pleasing and avoiding challenging your clients	Standing for your client's transformation and lovingly challenging them
Lack of self-worth in your pricing and offers	Surrendering to trusting the outcomes of your actions
Seeking validation or approval from others	Intuitive and connected to your inner guidance Authentic in self-expression; how you show up online is who you really are

Our healthcare system has traditionally been energetically gridded by the disempowered masculine programming that so often leads to burnout. Without proper breaks, long hours, and the need to override our bodies' natural functions (eating, going to the bathroom, having sunlight, and rest), the system is set up to fail.

The old paradigm of healthcare supports—

- Disempowered masculine programming
- Overriding your body's needs for breaks
- Profit and volume-based healthcare: how many prescriptions or vaccines you can give
- Suppression of your voice, needs, desires, or opinions as a practitioner

- Disconnection from self

The new Divine feminine paradigm of entrepreneurship supports—

- Operating your business through your empowered feminine essence
- Authenticity and self-expression
- Honoring your body's need for rest, bathroom breaks, food, water, etc.
- Heart-centered health care with more quality and focused time with the patient or client
- Connection to ourselves and inner healing so we can empower our patients

I call this Divine feminine archetype the "Queen." You *are* the Queen of your business, and this journey of you owning your brilliance to scale your business involves you *remembering* who you've always been to reclaim your crown. You don't need to be "better" or further along or have another certification to make an impact. You can step into this *now*.

The elevated Queen version of you—

- Owns your worth and knows what you bring to the table (your rare and regal soul gifts, your pricing, offers, etc.)
- Knows that you are an unlimited, powerful creator of your reality
- Sets healthy boundaries to keep your energy in pristine alignment to serve your clients
- Moves *first* and doesn't ask for permission to follow your desires
- Doesn't need validation because you are mission-driven and validate yourself. *You remember who you are*
- Is magnetic, drawing clients *into* your energy because you command your energy
- Is intuitive, following your own inner compass
- Operates from an expansive, abundant mindset

As a result, you operate your business from certainty, power, ease, and flow versus fear and force.

Moving from disempowered masculine programming into being the Queen of your business and embodying your Divine feminine essence *is* the transformation I take my clients into in all of my programs, retreats, courses, and 1:1 containers.

I give every single one of my clients a Queen crown to remember this. The crown represents two things—

#1. Your Divinity – The 7th chakra (crown chakra) connects us to the Divine and our intuition. I believe that if we connect to that Divine wisdom, we can channel it into our heart-centered businesses. When you do this, you use the gifts you were given and scale your profitable business.

#2. Your worth and value – You are inherently worthy and valuable just by BEING, by the way. We have all moved through challenges in our lives and businesses. You can choose to become bitter and stay small because of them or you can become empowered because of them. Your wounds don't make you unworthy; they are powerful portals of wisdom, knowledge, and power. By owning our stories, gifts, and experiences, we can step into greater potential, power, and prosperity.

Entrepreneurship offers a completely new way of operating and being in the world. However, when most pharmacist entrepreneurs come to work with me, they are subconsciously repeating the disempowered masculine programming, and it threads into their business.

For example, we're used to controlling everything in the pharmacy and having to be perfect. When you go to operate in your business, those controlling and perfectionist patterns actually hinder you. Practically, perfectionism often results in freezing and procrastinating because you fear making a mistake or your content not being good enough.

The old patterns you've learned over a lifetime now need to be unlearned so you can operate your business with more ease.

Leading your Divine feminine business involves a completely new way of BEING. It is not about the amount of action you take, but who you are being in that action. If you are running patterns of striving, proving your worth, suppressing your emotions to be productive, and trying to control everything in your business, you'll find yourself frustrated and burnt out.

This is why the inner transformation work is so important in shifting the way you operate in your business to experience more ease and flow.

When you're operating from Divine feminine leadership (Queen frequency) in your business, you are—

- Tuning in to your intuition and leading from your desires
- Setting healthy boundaries to protect your energy
- Radiating magnetism and certainty, which allows for natural client attraction
- Feeling all of the emotions that come up to be witnessed and moving through them as you step into your next level of income and impact
- Showing up authentically, shining your light as the real you in your self-expression and messaging—whether it's on social media, in person, or in leadership roles

When you have released the old programming, blocks, and blind spots that were keeping you gridded in the old disempowered masculine programming, your energy and power rise. When this happens, you begin taking empowered action and scale your business with ease and flow, being sourced from pleasure and what feels good for you.

So if HARD WORK + EFFORT = RESULTS isn't the answer to scale your business with ease and flow, what is?

The beautiful thing about owning your own business is that you're the one in charge calling the shots. And you get to decide how it gets to be for you.

If you want to scale your business with ease, the smoother path is to connect back with your body, desires, needs, and what lights you up. In other words: honor your desires, and take action on them. When you act on your desires, you're leading from *passion, excitement,* and what energizes you. Because you are *passionate* and full of energy, you'll naturally *energize* opportunities, money, clients, and infinite possibilities for your business.

Instead of plugging into the old paradigm of healthcare and thinking that HARD WORK = RESULTS, I want you to try this belief on.

Your DESIRE + DECISION = RESULTS.

Following your intuitive desires and taking action on them will lead to results. Every time. Why? Because you need to make lots of decisions as a business owner. If you aren't tapped into your desires, you don't know what you want or where you're going. If you're not taking action and making decisions, you're not moving forward, and you'll feel stuck.

Being tuned in to what feels good for your business is a skill that is learned over time. Trusting yourself and your intuition makes the path to success much smoother because you aren't second guessing yourself (which of course leads to procrastination, avoiding, etc., delaying your goals).

If all you have to do is tap into your desire and take action, why isn't everyone growing businesses? Simply put, we have subconscious resistance. Even though you might really want something on the conscious level, your subconscious mind is trying to protect you. In the next chapter, we will dive into overcoming this subconscious self-sabotage.

You may be wondering how YOU are different. Maybe this is one of the first times in your life where you are looking at your unique soul blueprint, gifts, and talents. I call this your Rare and Regal Soul Business Blueprint because your blend of gifts is **rare**: they are unique to *you*. They're also **regal** because your gifts are the expression of your royal Queen essence and embodiment.

The journal prompts that follow are designed to allow you to explore the *remembrance* of your gifts, life lessons, experience, and more that you'll be bringing into your business. I say "remembrance" because you knew when you came into this life what they are, but you need to recall them.

I want to go back in time with you to review your life and the fact that you've been preparing for this journey for a while now. Trust me, you'll see!

#1. *Follow these prompts to unlock your Rare and Regal Soul Business Blueprint*

Check off the items that you resonate with in the following chart, and write any others in the blank spaces.

A. Rare and Regal Soul Gifts

These are gifts you were born with, have had since birth, and expressed early on (before age 7) in your life.

Singing	Helping	Writing	Dancing	Nurturing/Supporting
Healing	Empathetic	Intuitive and highly sensitive	Teaching/ mentoring	Leadership
Compassion	Encouragement	Courage	Artistic/ Creative self-expression	Intelligence

What subjects did you excel at (or you were drawn to) in school?

- Math
- Science
- History
- Social Studies
- Music
- Art
- English
- Writing
- Language

- Technology

What specifically about those subjects intrigued you?
Ex: I always loved words and writing. I now use that in my business to help my clients communicate their brilliance and amplify their social media messaging for magnetic client attraction.

Your answers

_____
_____
_____
_____
_____
_____

B. Soul/Life Lessons

These are soul lessons that you've learned from certain past experiences that you can bring into your business. Journaling this helps you reflect on your resiliency and draws out the amplified gifts you bring to serve your clients.

Jot down your top three rock bottom moments and what the lesson was on the other side of it. Ex: I got kicked out of my house at age 23. The life lesson was to forgive my family, speak my truth, and take my power back. In turn, I now empower other pharmacists along their transformation journey. Repeated lessons often involve releasing judgment of some kind.

Memory #1.

_____
_____
_____

Soul Lesson #1.

_____
_____
_____

Memory #2.

_____

_____

_____

Soul Lesson #2.

_____

_____

_____

Memory #3.

_____

_____

_____

Soul Lesson #3.

_____

_____

_____

Some examples of life lessons:

- Forgiveness
- Patience
- Surrender and letting go
- Self-love
- Releasing judgment
- Healing
- Resiliency
- Flexibility
- Trusting yourself
- Speaking your truth
- Discernment
- Reclaiming your power

C. Proud Moments & Accomplishments

Allow yourself to acknowledge your life experiences and accomplishments. So often we down-play what we've done or simply forget how much we've been through and how resilient we are. List any experiences or accomplishments that made you feel fulfilled or proud of yourself and the subsequent empowering takeaway from it.

Proud Moment #1.

_____

_____

_____

Empowering Takeaway #1.

_____

_____

_____

Proud Moment #2.

_____

_____

_____

Empowering Takeaway #2.

_____

_____

_____

Proud Moment #3.

_____

_____

_____

Empowering Takeaway #3.

_____

_____

_____

Accomplishments—

- High school or college graduation
- Certifications or trainings you've moved through
- Health challenge you've overcome
- Volunteer projects you've contributed to
- Awards you've won
- Courses, programs, books, or businesses you've created
- Ideas or innovations
- People you've helped
- Papers you've written
- A proud moment in your life (getting married, having your children)
- Promotions you've had

Your Accomplishments

_____

_____

_____

_____

_____

_____

_____

_____

_____

_____

D. Leadership Experiences

Write down any other experiences that have shaped your journey as a leader.

Leadership Experience #1.

_____
_____
_____

Leadership Experience #2.

_____
_____
_____

Leadership Experience #3.

_____
_____
_____

Ex: I worked at my dad's pharmacy for 15 years and gained experience in customer service that I now use in my business.

#2. See if you can find threads of common themes in these experiences. These are SOUL lessons you are here to bring forth into your business.

We are looking for patterns to point back to your unique journey and how every experience has led you here right now.

These may have been repeated experiences you had that were the fertile training ground for your work as a leader and lightworker.

For example: You are here to reclaim your power, speak your truth, surrender control to trust, move from fear to faith, practice flexibility, etc.

Ex: I was often put in situations where I had to suppress my emotions and desires and give my power away to my family. One of the themes I've moved through is to reclaim my power.

You can utilize all of the above gifts, life lessons, experiences, certifications, and more to help your clients in their transformation.

These are some nontraditional ways I've unlocked and utilized my brilliance in my business—

- *I danced for 15 years when I was younger*...and when I host retreats I have my clients dance to release stuck energy and anchor into their confidence.
- *I always loved writing and the frequency of words*...and I now write books (like this one!) that empower, uplift, and inspire other women.
- *I was always intuitive and highly sensitive*...and now I'm able to use my intuition to help clients quickly release blocks to shift into their Queen embodiment.
- *I worked at my dad's pharmacy for years and developed the ability to connect with people very easily*...and now I am able to use those skills in my business to support my clients.
- *I was always drawn to science and physics*...and it lead me to study quantum physics, energy work, and alternative methods of healing.
- *I had traumatic experiences that broke me open to my life purpose*...and now I share my transformational story and help other pharmacists who feel stuck in their career to unlock their gifts to scale profitable heart-centered businesses.

In the Communicating and Delivering Your Brilliance chapter, I'll teach you how to articulate your brilliance in your messaging to attract your soul clients. Your soul clients will see you as the have-to-hire coach when they know, like, and trust you and see you showing up consistently and authentically.

Now that you've tapped into your gifts, experiences, and life lessons—aka your brilliance—your next step is to become aware of the subconscious fears that may block you from shining your light into the world.

**Bookmark this page as you'll be revisiting this later on in the book for the Communicating and Delivering Your Brilliance to Call in your Soul Clients chapter.

Step #1 Takeaways

#1. Leading your Divine feminine business involves a completely new way of BEING in your Queen frequency. Releasing disempowered masculine programming allows you to step into this Divine feminine essence.

#2. Anchoring into your Queen frequency involves—

- Tuning in to your intuition and leading from your desires
- Setting healthy boundaries to protect your energy
- Radiating magnetism and certainty, which allows for natural client attraction
- Feeling all of the emotions that come up to be witnessed and moving through them as you step into your next level of income and impact
- Showing up authentically, shining your light as the real you in your self-expression and messaging, whether it's on social media, in person, or in leadership roles

#3. Your brilliance = your soul gifts, life lessons, experiences, and accomplishments. When you unlock these gifts, you can use them in your heart-centered business to help your soul clients.

#4. Instead of HARD WORK = RESULTS, the new paradigm is DESIRE + DECISION = RESULTS

Journal Space

_____
_____
_____
_____
_____
_____
_____
_____
_____
_____
_____
_____
_____
_____
_____
_____
_____
_____
_____
_____
_____
_____
_____
_____
_____
_____
_____
_____

STEP #2. OVERCOMING SELF-SABOTAGE TO FEEL SAFE TO SHINE

You can have the best product, service, program, or course, but if no one knows about it, you won't be able to sell it. Even though you've tapped into your brilliance, you need to be able to communicate it to your audience to attract your clients and scale your business.

Self-sabotage is the most common barrier to scaling your profitable business. Your subconscious mind wants to keep you safe at all times, so when you're transitioning from your healthcare job to becoming an entrepreneur, so many blocks come up.

Your subconscious mind holds your beliefs, foundational programming, trauma, and blocks. Blocks are areas in your energy where you've subconsciously withheld your own love from yourself and/or prevented the love of others from getting through. Intuitively, blocks appear to me as dense black energies (or knots) in the aura, or energy field. Blocks are a result of emotions, beliefs, and energetic patterns that keep you safe, small, and protected and block the flow of energy. Your INTERNAL belief system creates your OUTER reality.

Examples of blocks include—

- Fear of being seen
- Imposter syndrome
- Procrastination
- People pleasing
- Analysis paralysis
- Perfectionism
- Unworthiness

- Overthinking
- Control patterns

As a result of past experiences, your subconscious mind creates protection mechanisms in the form of masks, armor, and defense mechanisms. These protection mechanisms are keeping you safe, but they are also guarding your heart from receiving in your business.

Examples of masks are –

- The Independent Woman Mask
    - You show up as being strong and not needing anyone because that would make you look "weak." In turn, you block receiving help, money, opportunities, and invitations to collaborate.
- Toxic Positivity Mask
    - You are always positive no matter what. You stifle your emotions and do not feel anything because it might derail your progress or productivity. As a result, you push yourself too hard and wind up burnt out.
- The "Good Girl" Mask
    - You are a "good girl" and do not know how to set healthy boundaries, speak your needs, or say NO. You people please and are nice, but it is not authentic because this is a protection mechanism to prevent people from being angry or upset with you. As a result, you only show positive emotions and people don't know the real you.
- Intellectual Mask
    - You are smart, and whenever someone meets you or talks to you, you share about your list of accomplishments as a way to prevent yourself from being truly vulnerable. As a result, people can't connect with you because you're in your mind instead of being in your heart CONNECTING with others.
- Funny Girl Mask
    - This is similar to the Intellectual Mask. You show up as funny and comical, but people don't know the real you because you're

uncomfortable with vulnerability. As a result, people can't truly connect with you.

Defense mechanisms like the masks/personas above prevent your clients and audience from knowing the real you. You present yourself on social media one way, but on the inside you may feel insecure, lost, or unworthy. Doing the inner transformation work in this book will help you get started on releasing the blocks, armor, and protection you've been operating with.

Here is how blocks are formed and how they practically impact your business. I'll use myself as an example.

I grew up believing I was not good enough because I was so sensitive. I always got in trouble for expressing my emotions, feelings, and needs. I created stories that I was unworthy of good things because I was "bad." When I was "bad," love was withheld from me, I was punished, or given the silent treatment. As a result, I held a lot of guilt and shame in my body and subconsciously punished myself through abusing my body, choosing unavailable men, and staying in abusive environments. My familiar identity was reinforced by the circumstances I attracted.

Here were my thoughts, beliefs, emotions, and patterns:

Thoughts and stories – "I am bad and unworthy of good things" "I'm not good unless I work hard and prove myself" "I'm too sensitive"

Emotions – Shame, guilt, fear

Patterns + Protection Mechanisms – Fear of being seen, imposter syndrome, perfectionism, people pleasing, control patterns, unworthiness

Masks + Persona – I was the "Good Girl" and Independent Woman and did not let people get close to me. Instead, I was judgmental, not trusting, and held people at a distance. My business growth suffered tremendously.

When it came to my business, I held unworthiness patterns in my energy and attracted clients who confirmed that belief system.

When you put yourself out there in your business, you'll often find your mind chattering away with incessant negative thoughts, and your body may literally freeze up. At one point in your life, it may not have been safe to speak your desires, share your thoughts, or shine your light.

These patterns impact every decision you make (or don't make) in your business.

For example, if you're used to people pleasing, you may be reserved in pricing/selling your offers because you're afraid someone will think you're greedy or that you're "taking" from someone. As a people pleaser, you may also abandon yourself when it comes to investing in yourself or working on your business.

If you're a perfectionist, you may wait until everything is "just right" before you go Live on Facebook, share your thoughts in a social media post, or launch your website.

Not only do you have all of these inner thoughts, beliefs, and patterns coming up from within you, you may also be protecting yourself to stay safe from the criticism of others and stifle your light and brilliance.

Some examples might be that you're afraid to shine your brilliance because...

- At one point it was not safe for you to be noticed or complimented
- Of your birth order – Ex: If you grew up in a big family and got lost in the crowd, if you were the youngest or middle child and didn't get noticed, or you were the oldest, but then felt dismissed when the other children were born. Maybe you didn't want to outshine your sibling, so you kept quiet, stayed small and hidden
- Cultural norms – you're not allowed to celebrate yourself or you feel you have to put your head down and just "work hard"
- Bullying or abuse – it's safer to go under the radar and stay small so you don't get picked on. This was how I protected myself—I made myself small so no one would pick on me or judge me.
- Getting rejected from parents, in dating, or by friend groups

- A critical parent never really SEEING you and your value or celebrating your gifts

There are so many nuanced memories that lead to self-sabotage patterns that can hold you back in your business. This is the deeper transformation work we dive into in Step into Your Queen: Elevate Entrepreneur Academy, where I share specific tools, strategies, and practices to help you calm your nervous system and anchor in safety so you feel safe to shine and scale your profitable business.

Often at the beginning stages of business, self-sabotage can be debilitating. But it doesn't have to be. You *can* move through this.

When you begin this deeper inquiry, be gentle and curious with yourself. You are waking up to parts of yourself that you may not be aware are operating within you.

Begin this inner exploration by asking yourself these questions to become curious about your current subconscious patterns.

1. What disempowering stories do I have about myself?
2. What (or who) was I not allowed to be or do when I was growing up?
3. What did parents/caregivers/society tell me I was not allowed to do?
4. What feelings resulted from that programming?
5. What are the primary patterns/blocks coming up in my business right now?

Journal Space

_____

_____

_____

_____

_____

_____

_____

_____

_____

_____

_____

_____

When you're holding onto blocks from the past, it is like holding onto a big anchor that is weighing you down. As you move through releasing these blocks by becoming aware of them, feeling the undigested emotions from your past, and reprogramming your subconscious mind, it frees up the energy for you to use in your business.

Move through this 3-step block clearing exercise to release subconscious fears and negative consequences of shining your light. By the way, you can change the initial sentence for whatever you are moving through. For example, instead of the negative consequence of shining your light, it could be, "What is the negative consequence of me being myself?"

My 3-Step Block Clearing Exercise

Let's start with this question to uncover your subconscious fears and negative consequences:

"If I made more money and impact and already had my dream goal inside my business, then _____."

Step #1. Write out some of the negative consequences of having more success in your business. Typically, our blocks are related to fears around how others will perceive us.

"If I'm TOO successful, wealthy, abundant...."

My partner...

- Will feel emasculated
- May leave me
- May resent me

I would...

- Be alone
- Attract haters and people who were jealous of me
- Lose my friends and family
- Feel guilty or ashamed

My parents...

- Will think I'm disrespecting them
- Will think I'm crazy/stupid/wrong for leaving my job
- Worked so hard for money that I can't possibly earn it with ease
- Will think I'm bragging

My coworkers...

- Will judge me
- Will ask, "Who the hell does she think she is?"
- May think I'm greedy
- Will be jealous of me

My clients...

- Will judge me for my prices
- Will judge my self-expression, lifestyle, or my offers
- May think I'm ripping them off

My friends and family...

- May feel threatened by my success
- May be jealous and move away from me
- May think I'm a rich snob
- May think I'm betraying them because I'm pursuing my dream
- Will judge/criticize me for my self-expression
- Will leave me

For example – You've identified your block as unworthiness and the negative consequence of being wildly successful is that you don't think you deserve it.

Who do you feel like you'd be betraying or feel guilty about outshining? Do you think you will attract haters?

Step #2. What has holding onto these stories been costing you?

- Money in my business
- Impact on my clients
- My mental and physical health
- Self-love and acceptance
- Connection and love
- Time with my kids
- Peace of mind
- Confidence and power

Ultimately, your subconscious mind is creating meaning around what will happen when you step out into this elevated identity, so it sabotages you. Some aspect of you will not feel safe if you step out and shine.

For each of the stories above, ask yourself what the worst case scenario in your mind will be if this happens. Fill out the chart below to get more clarity around it.

Person tied to the story	What I'm making it mean	How is this directly costing me in my business?	What is the truth?
#1.			
#2.			
#3.			
#4.			
#5.			

Step #3. Move through the list above and forgive each of the people involved, including yourself.

Forgive yourself and take radical ownership for creating these stories. Go through each person on the list and forgive them, too. You can even say the Hawaiian Ho'oponopono prayer—"I love you. I'm sorry. Please forgive me. Thank you."

You may be asking how this inner work shows up practically as tangible results. I'll tell you a story about one of my clients, Susan.

CLIENT STORY: Susan, Pharmacist and Health Coach

Susan is a brilliant pharmacist and health coach who came to one of my Elevate retreats and signed up for my Elevate program a couple years ago. She had many fears around shining her light, communicating her brilliance, and setting healthy boundaries in her business.

Her blocks presented as people pleasing, perfectionism, fear of being seen, imposter syndrome, and unworthiness. When she launched her program, she found herself freezing up when she had to talk about the investment level, share about her gifts, and communicate her brilliance.

As we started working together, I picked up that she had resistance around owning her pricing. Susan had a pattern of feeling responsible for how others perceived her and with her clients, this was no different. *These are subtle codependency patterns that were impacting her business growth.* She thought that once money was exchanged, she was responsible for getting her clients results.

As a result, she had been struggling to create results inside of her business to attract paying clients who wanted to work with her in her health coaching program.

When we started working together in a 1:1 capacity, I was guided to coach her around an experience that had happened in her childhood. We uncovered that she had early childhood experiences that made her freeze up in fear and quiet her voice. As a result of those experiences, she developed core beliefs that she had to make others happy to feel safe in her own body.

After moving through releasing and digesting the fears, anchoring in safety in her subconscious mind, and doing Inner Child work, she released these patterns and began to step into her power and shine in her business.

She went from hearing crickets in her first launch to creating a 5-figure launch after our work together!

This is the power of moving through these inner blocks and resistance so you can shine your light, your soul clients can connect with you, and you can scale your profitable business.

As you move through your business journey, these blocks may come up (and it's normal for them to.) You can come back to this exercise, be curious about why your subconscious is protecting you, and move through the release process with more ease and grace.

I challenge you to take these three action steps this week in your business to overcome blocks:

#1. Take imperfect action on something you've been avoiding. Need to follow up with your leads? Go do it. Need to launch your website? It doesn't have to be perfect. #DoTheDamnThing Queen! Head over to the Facebook group for support on this. We're there to cheer you on!

#2. Set the boundary you know you need to. Hang a sign on your door when you're working and need undisturbed time. Create time for your business. Say "NO" (with love of course) without explaining or over-apologizing.

#3. Say "YES" to your desire. Maybe it's finally investing in that coach you wanted to hire. Or hiring someone to help you clean the house. Say "YES" to your desires because when you do, you're really saying "YES" to yourself.

To go deeper into the themes in this lesson visit the *Scaling Your Heart-Centered Business Workbook* in the downloadable bundle.

Step #2 Takeaways

#1. Blocks are areas in your energy where you've subconsciously withheld your own love from yourself and/or prevented the love of others from getting through. Your INTERNAL belief system creates your OUTER reality. When you heal and release blocks, you become *lighter* and move forward in your business.

#2. The body is the subconscious mind, and past pain seeks protection in the form of masks, armor, and defense mechanisms. Working with your subconscious mind to release old programming and wire in new beliefs will help you create a new reality for your life and business.

#3. Moving through the three-step block clearing exercise will free up your energy so you can experience higher levels of abundance, joy, and expansion.

Journal Space

STEP #3. RELEASING MONEY MEMORIES TO RECEIVE ABUNDANTLY FOR YOUR GIFTS

Transitioning from being a healthcare worker to becoming a heart-centered entrepreneur involves a huge shift in how you relate to money. You're used to getting paid hourly in exchange for your time and getting paid every two weeks without question. Entrepreneurship is totally different, where you are deciding on your pricing, offers, packages, and how you attract clients. In essence, you have to sell yourself.

This is a huge shift for many HCPs as you create, package, and price your offers, packages, and sessions. You're advocating for yourself and your own worth and value when you share your pricing. Naturally, your relationship with money seeps through every aspect of your business.

Money blocks are a big barrier that I see pharmacists struggle with as they're launching and growing their businesses.

Money blocks like the ones that follow show up through old programming and beliefs—

- Unworthiness – *Who will buy my product/service? OR I can't possibly charge that!*
- Scarcity/lack – *I can't afford that OR I don't have enough _____(time/money) to do that.*
- Fear of investing in yourself – *I can't hire a coach until I make money in my business.*
- Imposter syndrome – *I'm not a REAL coach (I'm a beginner), so I can't charge full price yet.*
- Perfectionism – *I can't make money unless this offer, package, website is perfect.*

- Lack of belief in your ability to receive full payment for your gifts – *Bartering, discounting, or beta testing your programs.*
- Your pricing – *You price based on hourly rates or industry standards vs the potency of the transformation you bring to the table.*

Again, these are all normal ways of your subconscious mind protecting you ... but it's not serving you.

While you are used to getting paid on an hourly basis in traditional healthcare, entrepreneurship is completely different. Again, you get to decide your prices and the value you bring.

Instead of pricing based upon hourly rates, what everyone else is telling you to charge, or industry standard, I'm going to invite you to price based upon the potency of what you're bringing to the table. If you need a boost here to raise your prices, return to Chapter 1 where you can see your gifts and all that you bring to your clients.

Before you can start pricing your offers, you'll need to address your relationship with money.

Whether you are just starting or you've been in business for a while, there are stories tied to clients, money, and business in general that you may be holding on to. When you are holding onto stories tied to resentment, anger, shame, guilt, or other negative emotions, you are blocking your heart magnetism, money flow, and ability to receive for your gifts.

Imagine that every time you had a negative experience with money a part of your heart energy was blocked off—and that kept happening over and over again. To open your heart back up to receive, you'll need to release the stories and emotions blocking your magnetism.

Energetic Action Steps

#1. Make a list of negative experiences you've had around the following categories—

- Money
- Clients
- Business
- Coaches or other relationships (colleagues, family, friends)

Money

- Money stories your parents told you
- Beliefs you learned, heard, or absorbed growing up like, "It's not spiritual to want or ask for more because it means you're ungrateful" or "If I was really heart-centered, I'd charge less for my services"
- Seeing someone close to you get ripped off
- You got scammed out of money
- Bad experience with money or trusting someone with money
- You went bankrupt or have debt
- Negative experiences you had with money being stolen, taken, or borrowed but never paid back
- Someone under-delivered a service
- You got treated poorly or unfairly at a previous business/job
- Mistakes or investments that went south
- Lending someone money but never getting repaid (or seeing a close family member or friend have this happen)
- Judgments you have about others and their money (how they earn it, how much they make, etc.)

Business

- Someone complained about your service or product to you, your staff, or on social media
- Times you bartered with your business or took on a client just for the money even if it wasn't something that was aligned
- Giving away too much free content, not having boundaries, and feeling resentful
- Conversations you still replay in your mind from a past business experience
- Perceived business failures or bad investments

Clients

- Did a client ask for a refund or cancel working with you?
- Did you give over and beyond to a client, but they still had negative things to say?
- Does a previous client still owe you money that you never collected?
- Have you given so much to a potential client and felt resentful when they said they wanted help or your service, but then stopped messaging you when it came to taking action?
- Did you have a negative experience with someone who was a pain-in-the-butt client or someone who seemed to drain your energy?
- Has a previous client, lead, or prospect ghosted you?
- Are you resentful of any potential clients or leads you've invested time into only to have them say "no"?

Coaches or other Relationships (Colleagues, Bosses, Family, Friends)

- Did you have a coach who you had a falling out with?
- Did you have a negative experience with a coach that left you feeling disempowered, ashamed, or angry?
- Have you had a negative experience with a colleague?
- Have you had colleagues, family, friends, or other relatives say things about your business?
- Did a past boss say something about your work performance?

Anything that comes up here is valid and is coming up for a reason.

2. *Write down the disempowering stories you created about yourself, others, money, business, clients, or coaching relationships.*

Often we have absorbed imprinting from the world about these things. You may have subconsciously created beliefs about yourself or others when you experienced pain.

Ex: People can't be trusted. Money doesn't grow on trees. People take advantage of me.

 # 3. Move through each of these experiences and forgive.

When you choose to forgive, you are NOT forgiving the action or injustice. You are choosing to free yourself from the stories and meaning you've created around it along with how you may have taken it personally. Everyone is operating from their own lens, and often, people's conduct is a reflection of where they are in their own growth journey.

When you are able to forgive by seeing the situation, person, or entity from a higher perspective, everything shifts, and you're able to release the energetic charge around it.

Feel your feelings about this FIRST. Then move into a neutral space where you can see the situation from a higher perspective. *You can do this by listening to the Neutrality Meditation included in the Ascension Collection.*

If you have resistance to forgiving them, simply be *willing to* forgive.

Options to Forgive

#1. Move through each person on the list and say the Hoʻoponopono prayer to clear this.

Please forgive me. I love you. I'm sorry. Thank you.

#2. Listen to the Cord Cutting meditation in the Ascension Collection.

#3. Write a letter to the person who you feel the strongest emotion around. Express your feelings without filtering yourself, and after you've written it, you can burn it safely in a metal bowl or rip up the paper and throw it away.

You may be asking how this inner work translates to practical results in your business.

I want to share a practical example of one of my clients who had money fears, how she released them, and what her results were.

CLIENT STORY: Heather

Heather was a pharmacist and lifestyle coach who came into Step into Your Queen: Elevate Entrepreneur Academy wanting to call in more clients for her coaching business.

Her blocks were fear of being seen, perfectionism, unworthiness/shame, and fear of speaking up to embody her true self-expression. She had been telling an old disempowering story about "being bad and not worthy of good things" from an earlier experience in her adult life. As shown in David Hawkins's scale earlier in the book, shame is the lowest frequency the body can carry. If you're holding onto shame, you are severely diminishing your ability to receive good things into your life. This was Heather's case, too.

Her old money beliefs included "Money doesn't grow on trees," "I can't charge for my gifts," and "There is never enough." This was creating her reality of lack and scarcity in her business, resulting in a lack of clients and sales.

After moving through the first month of Step into Your Queen: Elevate Entrepreneur Academy, she released the feelings of unworthiness she had been holding onto for decades and got her first paying client! She went on to receive several more clients after that.

By the way, you can also attract money from multiple other sources. **Money can come to me in expected and unexpected ways** is a mantra I use often with my Step into Your Queen: Elevate Entrepreneur Academy clients. When you anchor in this belief, money can come to you from infinite sources.

Money is not just actual cash, but also anything of value that you are gifted.

Some examples of how this can show up—

- Being part of a referral or affiliate program
- Taking surveys to get paid for your knowledge

- Receiving passive income from creating a podcast or YouTube channel
- Paid partnerships for a product you believe in
- Receiving payments for writing articles for a magazine or organization
- Receiving a refund for an item
- Having someone gift you food, drinks, or anything else

See the Scaling Your Business Workbook in the downloadable bundle for more in-depth examples of this.

Be open to all the ways money in the form of actual cash, gifts, and value can show up for you.

Remember, it's your business, and you get to decide on your pricing, boundaries, standards, processes, and more. The next chapter, Communicating Your Brilliance, will tie everything together to deepen this exercise so you can get crystal clear on how you're creating life-changing results for your clients.

Step #3 Takeaways

#1. Money blocks show up when you have stories, beliefs, and negative emotions around experiences with money, business, clients, or other people. Holding onto these stories is costing you in your business and is like having a clogged pipe that won't allow money to flow to you.

#2. Releasing work will help you clear money blocks. The Ho'oponopono prayer, forgiveness, and cord cutting are examples of how to release resentment or other negative emotions to open your money channels.

#3. You can monetize your gifts to get paid abundantly for them in many different ways. Expand your traditional idea of receiving money to receive in a variety of ways.

Journal Space

STEP #4. COMMUNICATING AND DELIVERING YOUR BRILLIANCE TO CALL IN YOUR SOUL CLIENTS

Now that you've started to clear the most common blocks to shining your light and receiving for your gifts, you can move into feeling safe to shine and communicating and delivering your brilliance.

**Before you start on this chapter, revisit and reflect on your answers from Step #1. Unlocking Your Brilliance to see if any new insights came through as you moved through Steps 2 and 3. You'll bring what you unlocked in Step #1 into this chapter to communicate your brilliance.*

Communicating your brilliance comes down to sharing your gifts, self-expression, and light authentically, while articulating the magic and life-changing results you get your clients.

The deeper you go within yourself and healing your own heart, the deeper you can meet others. Your heart is your power portal and when you're authentically connecting back to this power center, it will magnetize your soul clients to you.

When you can share openly and *own* the transformation you've been through, it allows others to see all of you. If you find yourself shying away from this action, stop, and revisit the chapter Overcoming Self-Sabotage to Feel Safe to Shine.

This is about elevating your energy and owning your gifts and how you help your clients.

Some of the mistakes I see entrepreneurs making around authentically communicating your brilliance are—

- Vague communication in who you help and what the life-changing results are
- Coaching jargon without context of how you're helping them

- Only showing the highlight reel of your life vs connecting with them through authentic sharing of your story
- Lack of a framework to articulate how you are the bridge and result your client is looking for
- No clear calls to action or invitations to lead the person into an offer, program, or action step

This comes down to connecting back to your heart energy so your client knows you get them. Remember, empathy is the biggest needle mover for change.

For example, rather than saying, "I help ambitious women lose weight and gain more energy so they can live a life they love," you could say, "I help burnt out women in healthcare release the weight struggle so you can feel lit up from the inside out as you live with more ease and enjoyment."

It's specific and clear and instantly draws that person to you.

Some of the thoughts or blocks that may be coming up for you around communicating your brilliance might be:

- "Everyone knows this, why would someone pay me to coach them?"
- "There are SO many coaches out there, why would someone pick me?"
- "Someone can figure this out themselves or Google it."
- "I'm not unique enough."
- "I can't share about myself or my business because I'll be bragging if I do."
- "I'm just a beginner. I can't do this."
- "Even if I put my offer out there, who would buy my product/service?"

These are just stories and beliefs you have right now, and trust me, beliefs can be changed. (Insert sigh of relief.)

When you deeply *own* your brilliance and are embodied in your methodology, your rich and rare gifts, and how you help your clients transform and achieve results, your clients will *feel* that and trust you. But you have to know and trust yourself first.

These are questions to help you with that. Move through these questions to articulate how you help your clients on a deeper level and to communicate your true brilliance.

#1. What practical results/transformation do clients receive by being in my program?

For example, how are they *practically* going to shift by being in your program? What happens when a client moves through the program? Where do they start (Point A) and where do they wind up (Point B)?

Are they waking up feeling more energized to be able to play with their children and be present with their spouse?

Are they moving through their day with more ease, less anxiety, and more self-compassion?

The practical results/transformation clients receive in this program are....

_____

_____

_____

_____

#2. How is the client transformed by being in my energy?

You have an energy that people feel when they come to work with you. Do your clients feel calm, safe, and comforted? Do they feel energized, activated, and empowered? Get clear on what energy you bring to your containers.

_____

_____

_____

_____

#3. What are the life-changing, long-term results I bring to the table when a client hires me? How does this short-term investment create ripple effects in every area of their life moving forward?

Think of long-term results the client is receiving by moving through your program.

What will they walk away with that they can continue coming back to for years to come? This involves a shift from "What does this cost?" to "What is this investment providing me for the long haul?" This is how you build in value for your clients and affects how you communicate the potency of your pricing.

Ex: They get to plug into a system or strategies that they'll continue coming back to for the rest of their life. They get access to tools and shifts that will help them get back into alignment when they fall off course. They gain access to strategies that you've learned over X amount of years so they don't have to spend time Googling how to change on their own. They plug into a community of support so they don't have to move through the transformation alone.

#4. What gifts do I have that I bring to my programs? What are the unique gifts I bring to my clients that are unlike anyone else?

This is your chance to shine! Share about your methodology (the "what" not the "how"), your gifts, talents, and brilliance. Share about your journey, your story, struggles, and more! Your clients want to know the real you.

All of the above are valuable things your client wants to know about before they hire you.

Here are my unique gifts that clients get with me as an example:

#1. Laser-sharp intuition – I am able to quickly tune in to my clients to see their brilliance and help them articulate/communicate that to their audience to attract their soul clients. I'm able to clearly channel what wants to come through from Source to help my clients elevate their offers, pricing, standards, and messaging for magnetic client attraction.

#2. Collapsing and accelerating time – I am able to help clients collapse time by plugging them into strategies, systems, support, and shifts that I've learned over a lifetime and invested over $300,000 (aside from pharmacy school) in personal and business development. An outcome that would have taken them five years to figure out and achieve by themselves suddenly takes them six months.

#3. Rapid transformation – I'm able to help clients shift quickly, knowing the transformation tools and strategies that will help them elevate their energy and power to scale their business.

#4. Calibrating to Your Highest Queen embodiment – I see my clients' elevated Queen self and help them calibrate to that version of themselves very quickly. I'm also able to see the quickest, easiest path to their goal.

List the gifts you bring to your programs:

#1.

_____

_____

_____

#2.

_____

_____

_____

#3.

_____

_____

_____

#4.

_____

_____

_____

#5.

_____

_____

Now that you've identified your brilliance, you can begin to channel your offers.

Channeling your brilliance (your soul gifts, life experiences, lessons, and practical accomplishments) into deliverables for your clients to move through their transformation is how you begin receiving energy (money) for your gifts.

You can package and deliver your brilliance through offers in a variety of ways! I want you to really think outside the box on this one.

Remember, people are paying for you to help them collapse time and accelerate their path. Think of this example. Let's say you want to ship something in the mail. You arrive at the post office and want the package delivered overnight, it's going to cost more to get there quicker than if you wanted the ground shipping.

The same goes for how you can help your clients. People want services and products that make their lives easier, solve a problem they are having, and save time, energy, or money. Think of ways you can help your clients do one of the above and *share* about it!

In my 1:1 programs, I help my clients curate specific low-, mid-, and high-tier offers to sell to diversify their passive income and active income streams.

The following are different ways to deliver your transformation, depending on your personality, your business model, and how you love serving.

*Pro tip: Let this be easy for you. Don't feel like you *have* to create a membership just because someone else is. Decide based upon pleasure and what feels good and easy to you.

If you love—

- **Forming deeper relationships with your clients**, you can create an intimate Mastermind container to work with them for longer timeframes so you can go deeper with them. You can also create 1:1 containers to serve your clients on a deeper level for longer periods of time.

- **Connection and in-person experiences**, you can create an intimate in-person experience like a retreat or VIP day.
- **Having passive income and being able to duplicate your energy**, you can build an e-course or program where your client is digesting content and following certain action steps. Maybe you come on for a live call once a month with them.
- **Recording audios,** you can package meditations, audios, or hypnoses for clients to listen to.
- **Creating new content,** you can create a membership site, where you are adding in new monthly content.
- **Bringing people together virtually for shorter periods of time,** you can opt for a virtual experience like an online workshop, half-day retreat, or masterclass.
- **Writing,** you can create an e-book, PDF, or printed book.
- **Creating shortcuts for people,** you can create templates or PDF assets to sell.

I want to give you real-life examples of how this looks for me and for some of my clients.

I've created the following e-courses, programs, books, PDFs, retreats, meditation bundles, etc.

- **The Ascension Collection** – A compilation of over 40+ meditations, activations, and hypnoses to help you elevate along your ascension journey. *You receive this free as part of the Book Bundle when you scan the QR code at the beginning or end of this book.*
- **The Elevate Membership** – A soul-nourishing 12-month membership to help you release blocks holding you back so you can elevate your reality and own your brilliance.
- **Monetize Your Magic e-course** – A six week e-course to help you launch your profitable, heart-centered business.
- **Queen, Unlocked** – A four-week 1:1 deep dive to help you unlock and rise into your Queen embodiment. We dive into inner child healing, subconscious clearing, reclaiming your power, setting sacred boundaries,

and more to help you elevate into unshakeable confidence and power as you scale your business.

- **Step into Your Queen: Elevate Entrepreneur Academy** – My signature six-month program to help you transform from burnt out pharmacist to lit up full-time entrepreneur, scaling your profitable heart-centered business. We move through releasing self-sabotage, elevating your energy and power, and clearing money blocks and subconscious programming.
- **Release and Rise Program** – A six-month group program to help women release blocks to rise into your highest embodiment.
- **Magnetic Wealth Queen** – My most intimate eight-month 1:1 program to help you own your brilliance and magnetism to scale your profitable heart-centered business to six figures and beyond. I help you create an energetically sustainable business without burnout or overwhelm.
  - We move through helping you deeply own your soul gifts, unlocking and holding higher levels of wealth and clients, creating soul-led offerings, and developing your profitable product suite to create a pleasure-led business from ease and flow.
- **The Elevate Retreat** – A three-day in-person experience to help pharmacist entrepreneurs embody their feminine magnetism to scale their profitable business.
- **My previous four books** – *Revealing Your Inner Radiance: Healing through the Heart*; *Reclaim Your Power: A Roadmap to Re-energizing Your Life*; *Lighten Up: 7 Weeks to Release, Recharge, and Revitalize*; and *Embracing Your Light as a Highly Sensitive Person: A Guide to Developing Your Empathic Gifts*

Here are some real-world examples of how I've helped my clients monetize their brilliance.

CLIENT STORY: Rachel

In her own words, here is Rachel's story and how we worked together to monetize her gifts.

"For my business, book club (Invigorate), and all of the workshops and presentations I've created, I combined my love of teaching, coaching, and personal growth with my performance, public speaking, and writing gifts. For my sound bowl offers, I combined my love of music, prayer and meditation, and performing with my faith and spirituality."

Invigorate: Attuning to Your Best Life – An eight-week e-course designed to bring awareness to six key areas of life (work/purpose/passion, self-love, health, relationships, abundance, and joyful activities/adventure/attitude). In this course, participants identify which parts of their lives are nourishing and draining and use this information to set clear goals and make improvements to help them maximize their potential and live their best life.

Minding Your Mind Presentation/Workshop – A two-hour presentation/workshop that teaches about the importance of self-care and how our mindset affects all areas of our lives.

Sound Bowl Guided Meditations for the Soul – A collection of 12 recorded guided meditations accompanied by soothing crystal sound bowls. This includes journal prompts for each meditation.

Sound Bath Sessions – Customized crystal sound bowl sessions, sometimes combined with yoga and reiki from other practitioners to help calm the nervous system and restore peace and balance in the body.

CASE STUDY: Katie Wood – Fertility Coach + CEO of Pharm to Wellness

In her own words, here is Katie's story and how we worked together to monetize her gifts.

"Experiencing my own fertility struggles brought me awareness, empathy and compassion in this space. I have always had a curiosity for nutrition and healthy living, but knowing that we have the ability and power to create generational change for our children and our children's children through OUR food and lifestyle choices … Well let's just say that really stuck with me and lights me up, and it's my mission to share this message and mindset."

Naturally Nourishing Fertility 1:1

An intimate 1:1 coaching container where my client and I work closely together on a bi-weekly or monthly basis and dive into nutrition, overall health and lifestyle (sleep, stress, self-care, etc.) to nourish their mind and body for a calm, confident and joyous fertility and pregnancy journey.

Confident Conception Workshop

A 90-day hormone workshop where clients get weekly modules and worksheets on a new topic each week, all to support balanced hormones and optimized fertility.

Confident Conception Membership

A six-month membership that comes with monthly themes and includes foundational modules, videos, worksheets and a private, members-only Facebook group for monthly group coaching calls and weekly question threads.

Conscious Conception

A meditation bundle to support the mind-body connection and visualization, illuminate abundance, and reduce stress.

Feminine Prescription

Personal essential oil roller blends are intuitively curated with hormones, fertility, and women's health in mind.

Fruitful Fertility 101

A PDF guide that outlines the essentials of preparing your body for a fruitful fertility journey from knowing how to track your fertility to picking out the right supplements and nourishing your body with fertility-boosting foods.

What resonates from the above that you'll create for your business? Journal your ideas here.

_____

_____

_____

_____

_____

Step #4 Takeaways

#1. Communicating your brilliance to magnetize your soul clients requires tapping into your heart and speaking from a space of empathy where you "get" what your soul client is moving through.

#2. You can choose new money beliefs and to elevate your pricing based on the potency of the transformation you offer.

#3. Being clear in how you communicate your brilliance, having clear calls to action in your posts, and having frameworks to clearly share about how you help your clients get results will help you draw in people who you can serve.

Journal Space

_____
_____
_____
_____
_____
_____
_____
_____
_____
_____
_____
_____
_____
_____
_____
_____
_____
_____
_____
_____
_____
_____
_____
_____
_____
_____
_____
_____

Step #5. Systems, Structure, Support to Scale Your Profitable Business

We've just moved through four foundational steps of scaling a profitable business.

Step #1. Unlocking Your Rare and Regal Soul Gifts + Becoming the Queen of Your Business

Step #2. Overcoming Self-Sabotage to Feel Safe to Shine

Step #3. Releasing Money Memories to Receive Abundantly for Your Gifts

Step #4. Communicating and Delivering Your Brilliance to Call in Your Soul Clients

All of those elements are important, and the final step is having the masculine structures, systems, and support to be able to energetically hold the clients and wealth you desire.

You can't have the feminine desire without a masculine container or structure. You need both.

As a practical example, imagine a bottle of water. Now imagine it without the masculine structure of the actual water bottle. The water would spill all over the place, right? The same goes for your business. You can have all of the desires in the world, but if there is no clear channel (in the form of an offer, product, or service) for your energy to move into, your clients won't know how to work with you.

To hold more clients and money (energy), you'll need masculine structures to lead them into an offer or program. When you have the systems, structure, and support, you can expand and scale your business. The more you can focus your energy on your zone-of-genius while having systems in place, you'll be able to scale with ease and flow instead of feeling scattered or overwhelmed.

The following questions/prompts will help you create masculine structures to hold higher levels of wealth and clients. *You will find more in depth action steps and space for journaling in the Scaling Your Business Workbook in the downloadable bundle.*

Journal prompt questions to ask yourself—

These are all questions that YOU get to decide on—as the Queen of your business.

Structures

#1. What is your Signature offer/program that you lead your clients to?

- Who is it for?
- At what point of their journey are they coming to you to be able to enroll in the program?
- What is their starting point (Point A) when they join and what does the end of the transformation (Point B) look like when they are complete with your program? Point A = their pain points, struggles, and challenges. Point B = their transformation, desired results, and end point.
- What is the pricing of the offer?
- What is the length of time for the program?

_____

_____

_____

_____

_____

#2. What energetic boundaries do you have around your business? **You'll find more in-depth information on this topic in the Scaling Your Business Workbook in the downloadable bundle.

- What days/times do you work? When do you shut down for the day?
- When do you see clients? How often (weekly, biweekly)?
- What are the boundaries around who you get on a Discovery Call with and offer your program to?
- What are the qualities of your soulmate client? *You get to decide who you work with!*
- How do you communicate with your team? How often?

_____
_____
_____
_____
_____

#3. Client Communication

- Who gets access to your energy? Do you allow all clients (even those in group programs) to access you via Messenger or is it reserved for 1:1 clients?
- What boundaries do you have for clients to communicate with you? Through email, Messenger, Voxer? Do you give out your personal cell phone or home phone number?
- What are your office hours and response times to emails or messages?
- How often are your clients able to contact you? *You can set limits. You don't have to be available at all times.*

_____
_____
_____
_____
_____

Streamlining Systems + Processes

Client Processes

- What does your enrollment process look like? Do you have your clients sign a contract?
- What is the onboarding and offboarding process?
- How do you collect payments? How do you handle failed payments?
- How do you handle refund requests?

Team Processes

- Do you delegate to your team to handle these back-end processes? Which ones?
- How does your team communicate with you? Voxer, Messenger, through a software platform like ClickUp?

Marketing Processes

- When and how are you posting on social media or YouTube, sending a newsletter, etc.?
- How often are you showing up on these channels?
- Is there a process for repurposing or cycling content?

_____
_____
_____
_____
_____

Support

Business Support

Who is supporting you? Are you doing all of the things in your business? The more intentional Divine masculine support you have, the more your feminine Queen essence can expand.

Think about tasks that you do on a weekly basis that you can delegate to someone else.

- Virtual assistant who can help you create Canva images, schedule client calls, take care of onboarding processes, publish your blog or newsletter, etc.
- Social media/marketing support to create images, post content, repurpose content across social media channels
- A coach/mentor who you work with to guide you with shifts and strategies to scale your business, help you with your mindset, and release blocks holding you back
- Accounting support to help file your taxes, do bank reconciliation, or optimize your profit margin
- Small business lawyer to help you draw up client contracts or submit a trademark request
- Web designer to support you with back-end processes like SEO optimization or to ensure your website is running smoothly

_____
_____
_____
_____
_____

Tech Support

**Please see referral trial links for your tech support in the Scaling Your Business Workbook in the downloadable bundle.*

What tech support do you need to scale your business?

- A place to host your course or program content, Ex: Kajabi, Teachable
- Recording or broadcasting videos, Ex: Camtasia, Ecamm Live, or Streamyard
- Booking link for a Discovery call, Ex: Calendly
- Newsletter software, Ex: Constant Contact, Aweber, Mailchimp

- Software to create social media images, Ex: Canva
- Storing files, Ex: Dropbox, Vimeo

_____
_____
_____
_____
_____

You need BOTH feminine desire and pleasure-led ACTION to materialize the outcomes you want for your business. If you have the desire, but never act on it, it won't materialize. If you have no clarity or direction, you'll be swirling in random action or INACTION.

Having clear systems, structures, and support will help you focus on your zone-of-genius and scale your profitable business.

It's allowed to be EASY and it's YOUR time to SHINE, Queen!

Step #5 Takeaways

#1. When you have clear systems, structures, and support to help you scale, your business will run smoothly. It's allowed to be easy, Queen! The more you can lean on masculine support, the more your business (and feminine Queen essence) will expand.

#2. Having clear boundaries around your energy will help you focus on your zone-of-genius and be present and productive.

#3. The more CLEAR you are on these processes and systems, the smoother your business will run.

You've moved through each of these steps and have seen the power in doing both the inner transformation work AND implementing the practical strategies to scale your business.

Over the last decade, I've helped thousands of healers in health care scale heart-centered businesses.

These are a few of the types of coaches and healers I have helped:

- Anxiety Coach
- CBD Consultant
- Fertility + Pregnancy Coach
- Functional Medicine Coach
- Health and Wellness Coach
- Holistic Oncology Coach
- Holistic Health Coach
- Hypnosis Practitioner
- Life Coach
- PCOS Coach
- Self-care Coach
- Self-love Coach
- Stress Management Coach
- Spiritual Life Coach
- Weight Loss Coach
- Women's Empowerment Coach
- AND MORE

You don't have to do this alone, Queen. There are thousands of other pharmacist entrepreneurs in my community who want to support you and watch you shine!

Here are your next steps along your journey—

#1. First, I want you to take advantage of the **Step into Your Queen: Scaling Your Heart-Centered Business Trainings + Workbook** from the downloadable bundle where I'll take you through shifts, structures, systems, and support along your journey.

In this BONUS content, you'll find the trainings and PDF guide with:

- Over 40+ subconscious programming audios to help you step into your Queen embodiment
- Specific journal prompts to support you in releasing blocks keeping you stuck
- Energetic management tools to calm your nervous system to feel safe to receive
- Money mindset shifts and affirmations to help you anchor into more confidence, power, and abundance to elevate your business success
- Structures, systems, and support to help you scale your heart-centered business
- Practical needle mover action steps to help you elevate into entrepreneurship
- Business and technical support recommendations to scale with ease

To access your free Trainings + Workbook, open your camera app on your phone, and hold your camera over the QR code. Click on the link that appears, and you'll be brought to a page to enter your name and email to receive this free BONUS resource!

#2. If you already know you want to dive into this work, I've curated specific support in my Step into Your Queen: Elevate Entrepreneur Academy to help you scale your profitable healing business.

In Step into Your Queen: Elevate Entrepreneur Academy, I help you with the SHIFTS, STRATEGIES, and SUPPORT to:

- Release blocks (imposter syndrome, perfectionism, people pleasing, etc.) keeping you small and stuck so you can shine in your brilliance, calling in your soul clients with ease and flow
- Neutralize money stories and unwind unworthiness so you can expand your receiving capacity for higher levels of wealth and clients
- Elevate your energy and power to feel safe to take consistent action to scale your profitable heart-centered business

This six-month program is for female healers in health care who...

- Have been in business for at least six months and have a Signature Offer to sell
- Are ready to invest in yourself to scale your profitable healing business
- Are committed to showing up fully to this program to release blocks and own your brilliance
- Have a big vision and deep desire to serve your community using your soul gifts and get paid abundantly for them

If this is YOU, I'm inviting you to explore Step into Your Queen: Elevate Entrepreneur Academy!

If you have any questions, I'm happy to help! Please email me at christina@pharmacistcoach.com to learn more and feel this out together.

You'll be plugged into a proven system that I've mapped out over the last 10 years of being an entrepreneur and scaling my business to seven figures. You'll be supported by dozens of pharmacist entrepreneurs who get you and want to see you SHINE!

To learn more about Step into Your Queen: Elevate Entrepreneur Academy, scan the QR code here.

Journal Space

_____
_____
_____
_____
_____
_____
_____
_____
_____
_____
_____
_____
_____
_____
_____
_____
_____
_____
_____
_____
_____
_____
_____
_____

STORIES OF HEART-CENTERED HEALERS IN HEALTH CARE

Before we dive into the stories of these amazing heart-centered women, I want to tell you something about them. These are powerful heart-centered healers who I have had the privilege of getting to know on a deeper level through this book project. Many of them are or have been my 1:1 or Step into Your Queen: Elevate Entrepreneur Academy clients, attended Elevate retreats, and even contributed to past books. I have been a humble witness to their transformation.

I am proud of say that our contributing authors span across various ethnicities, cultures, backgrounds, and experiences. You'll see aspects of yourself in all their stories. Follow them. Friend them on social media. They're your biggest cheerleaders.

I'm incredibly honored and humbled to have had the opportunity to work closely with these women who are beacons of light in the world. I'd like to introduce these 19 women!

Holistic Health Coaching

Dr. Sarah Shore Anderson is the founder of ThriveRx Consulting, LLC. She designs clinical teams and strategy for novel, collaborative wellness solutions within health tech start-up companies. She utilizes her background in leadership, health coaching, managed care pharmacy, pharmaceutical outcomes, and global health and wellness engagement in the development of integrative, pharmacist-led services.

Through her partnerships, she cultivates innovation leading to a meaningful impact in the industry. Previously, she created a managed care pharmacy residency program and pharmaceutical outcomes clinical manager position at Medica Health Plans and developed the pharmacist health coach role at RedBrick Health/Virgin Pulse. Dr. Sarah has a doctor of pharmacy degree with an emphasis in leadership from the University of Minnesota and is a nationally board certified health and wellness coach, as well as a holistic clinical herbalist.

Dr. Sarah can be found at www.thriverxconsultingmn.com

Trials + Testimony into the Entrepreneurial Journey

As we learn, grow, and evolve, we will have successes worth celebrating and failures worth reflecting on, one day realizing that our less-than-ideal happenings open doors to next steps on our career journey. I took a year off after undergrad, as I was initially placed on the ranked waiting list for pharmacy school. This hiccup, unknowingly at the time, sparked the beginning of my entrepreneurial journey.

I was trained and worked as a health and wellness coach at a health insurance company, and this experience shaped my career trajectory in ways I never could have imagined. That experience and the connections I made that year paved the path for me to develop a managed care pharmacy residency program and ultimately led me to innovate in the global health and wellness space by creating the pharmacist health coach role.

Through these past experiences, I have come to realize that sometimes bad luck is actually good luck in disguise. The key isn't to wait for luck. The key is to make your own luck and find a sense of agency within yourself to say "yes" to circumstances that present themselves.

I thank my mom for instilling in me an inner sense of self-assurance. Speaking of my mom . . . while I was in pharmacy school, my mom unexpectedly passed away. This life-changing time in my life triggered me to evaluate and reflect on my values, purpose, and priorities and highlighted the importance for me to create alignment and harmony amongst my personal and professional goals.

The entrepreneurial work I am doing allows me to be wholeheartedly present with my kids AND create an impact in the profession of pharmacy. We can use the wake of a tragedy to reimagine better versions of ourselves and reinvent ourselves. I saw firsthand, throughout my mother's journey with multiple sclerosis, how important lifestyle factors, mindset, and attention to dimensions of wellbeing are to living well with a chronic illness. Contributing to the development of new products, services, and technology, which are grounded in taking a whole-person approach, and seeing the positive outcomes experienced by users propels me forward as I continue down this path of entrepreneurship.

Share Your Brilliance

As a stimulator (my result from the StandOut Assessment), I bring energy and inspiration to innovative organizations whose mission and vision I am passionate about impacting. As a connector (my other result from this test) with a very detailed memory (I swear due to playing the memory game with my mom *ad nauseum*!) and strength of individualization, I can readily forge connections amongst both people and concepts, in unique ways, whether to solve problems, remedy a challenging situation, or enliven a cause.

My fundamental belief in abundance and gift of maximizer (my result from the StrengthsFinder assessment) inspires others to do more with what they have, whether money, resources, talent, or ideas. As a generator (again from StrengthsFinder), I remain open to new opportunities, having faith that whatever is attracted to me—whether work, relationships, good fortune—is present for a reason. Through my ThriveRx Consulting business, I design clinical teams and strategies for innovative, collaborative wellness solutions within health tech start-up companies. I utilize my background in leadership, health coaching, managed care pharmacy, pharmaceutical outcomes, and global health and wellness engagement in the development of integrative, pharmacist-led services.

Overcoming Challenges to Scale

Embracing ambiguity and imperfection along with acknowledging that I needed to create space in my life for growth and development were key to my moving forward with leaving my job as coaching team manager at a global health and wellness company. Through participating in a local, community-based leadership program, I became more self-aware of what drives and motivates me—being able to serve, make an impact, and experience the ideal.

My interest and desire to wear multiple hats as well as be able to utilize skills from my vast background, made it difficult for me to narrow my initial focus for my business. The more that I talked with other like-minded entrepreneurial healthcare professionals and took time to listen to my heart, the more I realized that the business I am currently attracting—working with health tech start-up companies on strategy—is what I am meant to focus on right now. I have learned many life lessons through parenting, death of loved ones, and creating each position I have held thus far; these lessons include letting go, realizing that done is better than perfect, and uncovering that with patience, resilience, and faith, I can fearlessly "go rogue" and find deep satisfaction in life when flowing with what the present has to offer.

Monetizing Your Healing Gifts

I am currently working with a health tech start-up company to build their clinical team and design features and processes to support their app product. I co-host a podcast and have contributed to a couple of white papers in the virtual care space. I am developing sales material for a new service being offered by a virtual functional medicine group. I serve as a preceptor for pharmacy students and guest lecturer for a health coaching elective course. My speaking engagements include being a PED-X speaker (giving a TEDx type talk to pharmacy students), giving a keynote address at my alma mater's leadership emphasis area graduation, and speaking at local pharmacist association annual meetings.

What Lights You Up About Your Business

Working with visionary groups of people who think outside of the box and are interested in working collaboratively to enhance their mission lights me up. Blending pharmacists' knowledge with health coaching strategies and curating new products and services within the health and wellness space to ultimately improve the lives of others is my calling. I am passionate about this work as it facilitates expansion and awareness of nontraditional pharmacist roles, and ultimately, enriches the lives of those who utilize the products, services, and technology to support them in thriving.

Advice Along the Journey

Make a commitment to yourself to act if you find that your work is no longer in alignment with your values, or you feel you have lost your sense of purpose. There is power in choice. You can choose to stay stuck, or you can choose to be bold and courageous. Put yourself out there ... do not wait for an invitation. Network and leverage your connections to co-create synergy and enrich each other's work and lives. Just as going through pharmacy school takes tenacity, grit, grace, patience, sacrifice, and courage . . . so does this journey we are all on to find soul-fulfilling work.

Share your vision, feel empowered to ask for what you need, showcase what you have to offer, go rogue occasionally, pitch a proposal for an idea that could fill a gap, solve a problem, or add value in a new way; you are your own best advocate. Take time to revel in the unpredictable and wonder-filled twists and turns of life that make you who you are today. There is an abundant need for you and your unique talents. Keep shining YOUR light, whether it be a fierce flame or gentle glow. Both individually and collectively, we make a difference in this world.

What it Means to Be a Heart-Centered Healer in Health Care

The opportunity to thrive abounds when people feel supported, engaged, and empowered with their health. Focusing on partnerships and relationships while contributing to tools that will revolutionize healthcare brings health and healing to individuals, communities, and populations of people; what a joy! Being a heart-centered practitioner in the healthcare space means I utilize my strengths daily and feel alignment amongst my values and priorities ... living life full out with purpose and intention.

Dr. Marina Buksov is a holistic pharmacist, health coach, herbal educator, and lifelong learner of the healing arts. She is the creator of the Build Your Holistic Herbal Practice course, mentoring other healthcare professionals in clinical herbal and business skills. She is also a functional medicine pharmacist as part of the PharmToTable telehealth platform.

Dr. Marina guides pharmacists to rediscover their passion for medicine by expanding their mind and clinical skills to include natural, holistic, alternative and herbal medicine from which pharmacy originated in the first place! She believes that pharmacists can step into purpose and service by supporting and inspiring whole body health.

When she is not working or studying, Dr. Marina likes to dance, paint, and tinker with various concoctions (tea blends, meals, DIY projects). She lives with her husband, two adorable kiddos, and two mischievous kitties in NYC.

Connect with Dr. Marina at drmarinabuksov.com.

Trials + Testimony into the Entrepreneurial Journey

The seed for my entrepreneurial journey was planted when I was finishing pharmacy school, but it was a long and winding road for a number of years.

The ultimate turning point for when I finally committed to my business was also the breakthrough to monetization. It all came down to a single decision. My coach, Dylan, asked me to consider putting my business at the forefront as Plan "A" instead of keeping it on the back burner. So I recorded a selfie-video of my present self, reminding my future self of my "why."

Being both a patient in our current health model and having been trained in both Western and Eastern medicine, I serve as a bridge for others. I am a voice for the sustainable and conservative use of resources to preserve our health and livelihood on a grand scale and for generations to come. I advocate for taking our power back as practitioners—and patients with body autonomy and self-care—as citizens and stewards of this abundant planet.

Leading with the "why," I realized I was not going to let any setbacks stop me. Instead, I'd find a way to keep going and build the business and life I am capable of creating and worthy of having.

Share Your Brilliance

Often feeling misunderstood and different growing up, I dove into a lot of self-help books, and later invested in coaching through my various blocks. In addition, I encountered various life events and health challenges on my journey to entrepreneurship. I came to see that each setback actually presented an equally charged opportunity to learn, overcome, and grow.

Each level of my personal evolution corresponded to more alignment with my true calling. I had to fight my ego's need for control, my yearning to be liked, my unworthiness patterns … and learn to surrender and find self-reliance and self-love. And I admit it is still a work-in-progress most days! But now, I get to share these profound lessons with my clients and my students.

I realized that my personal strengths and gifts lie in being highly empathic and compassionate, having drive and resilience, and seeing the big picture. Combined with organizational and leadership skills and the desire to lead a life of service and integrity, I have transformed my gifts, skills, and life lessons into my mentorship business model.

Overcoming Challenges to Scale

Entrepreneurship did not come easily or intuitively to me because I was never encouraged to go in this direction, nor was it mirrored to me by those around me. From a young age, I was taught to follow the straight and narrow, so I learned to achieve a certain level of results that were expected of me. It became easy to associate my accomplishments with a feeling of external validation. In a way, it was a strategy to avoid any "risky business" ... but it also kept me playing small for a long time.

However, the security and surefootedness of following a "safe" path virtually dropped out from under my feet when it came time for me to graduate pharmacy school and start my career. Suddenly, the systematic roadmap of how many credits and exams I need to check off was gone. As I became crippled with indecision about my next steps, my confidence plummeted and my body started manifesting dis-comfort and dis-ease as a result. I progressively developed various intestinal disorders, adult onset acne, PCOS, and dacryostenosis.

For the first time in my life, I looked within for answers. Before this point, I always turned to an outside authority: my parents, my teachers, my doctors, my peers, my friends. I was invited to look within by one of my pharmacy school professors and mentors, Dr. Vibhuti Arya. This became permission for exploration of the unpaved, less traveled journey that beckoned me. I realized that I didn't know exactly what my calling was back then, but I did know that I was not aligned with the trendy, shiny, and respectable career paths that I was feverishly applying for at the time.

So instead of committing to a path that I was convinced would make me miserable, I bought myself time by taking a local retail job in community pharmacy. By a stroke of (bad/good?) luck, that position fell through, and I ended up finding employment in a pharmacy that specialized in traditional Russian herbal medicine. I was then connected to Christina, who sparked my interest in health coaching, and later supported my decision to follow my heart and enroll in herb school. From there, I continued to break through the mental patterns and health struggles that held me back to build my business part-time and finally transition to full time as of this year.

Monetizing Your Healing Gifts

My money-magic momentum picked up when I followed a specific plan to structure and streamline my business, with a focus on income-producing activities, as guided by my coach, Joey. I quickly took the necessary action steps to validate my business idea, create an exciting offer, and conduct a social media launch ... all before actually building the program that had only existed in my mind at the time. When I collected my first client's payment, it became real. And I quickly filled a few more spots and set a start date.

Each business endeavor is a wild and exciting ride. To date, I have created a mix of high- and lower-ticket products and services, in the format of self-paced, real-time, virtual and in-person classes, workshops, 1:1 and group programs, as well as hand-made custom herbal tea blends. Last year I ran my first retreat, in the middle of a pandemic, and international to boot!

What Lights You Up About Your Business

Looking back, I don't know how I managed to create, prepare, and execute my first big program curriculum between my full time job and family responsibilities. But I was inspired, and suddenly, it was exciting to do the work. I hired a graphic designer, and she helped me transmute my vision from my mind's eye into reality. Since I was creating the teaching materials in real time, I had to stay at least one week ahead of schedule at all times, which required me to prioritize tasks with absolute precision and organized focus.

I realized that researching, organizing information, and presenting it in a digestible manner is both a strength and a passion of mine. It brings me joy to help people cut the learning curve and empower themselves with knowledge and skills. I love witnessing the subtle shifts that later turn into huge transformations for my clients. I am overjoyed and super proud of their accomplishments and love both celebrating their wins and cheering them on in their next endeavors.

Advice Along the Journey

I encourage aspiring entrepreneurs to start their business from a place of empowerment and desire. Understanding their own "why" and that they are choosing to embark on their mission and do the work will continue to inspire and motivate them along the way, even when challenges inevitably arise.

What it Means to Be a Heart-Centered Healer in Health Care

It means treating the person in front of me with the utmost humanity and dignity. Serving is not about inflating one's own ego or earning validation. It is only about them: the client. It is impossible to serve everyone, so I focus on finding those clients I can truly serve from a place of love rather than to fulfill some need on my end, monetary or otherwise.

Jenna Carmichael, PharmD, and founder of Wobbly Arrow Wellness is a holistic oncology pharmacist and health coach. She works with women who are looking for a new perspective on wellness during their cancer journey. Dr. Jenna has over ten years of pharmacy experience, most of that time working with cancer patients. As a board-certified oncology pharmacist, she started a telemedicine clinic in a rural health system focusing on symptom management. She has certifications in yoga, reiki, meditation, pharmacogenomics, and intuitive healing to give her clients access to a full 360-degree view of health. Dr. Jenna believes in the power of food and stress management strategies as key foundational components for health and wellness. For more information, go to www.bio.site/wobblyarrow.

Trials + Testimony into the Entrepreneurial Journey

I'm a pretty typical product of the 1980s. My mother told my sister and me that we could be anything we wanted and we could have it all ... but we had to work for it. Growing up, a few events helped shape who I am now—my parent's divorce, becoming ostracized from my high school group of friends after a car accident, and studying abroad in Italy. I fell in love with the laid-back Italian lifestyle but did not embody that easy-going way of life and found myself caught up in the hustle and bustle of life once I returned to the States and went to pharmacy school. After two residencies, I landed what I thought was my perfect job—one I created from my residency project. I built a telemedicine clinic for cancer patients taking oral chemotherapy (a brand new form of treatment back in 2012). Over the next five years, the clinic grew to three pharmacists, one assistant, and over 1,000 patients. I also was the residency director and a clinical researcher. I realized that I never slowed down after Italy, almost ten years later. I was still in fight or flight, student mode—work and getting the next achievement was more important to me—but soon burnout took over.

Underlying all this was a deep-seated unworthiness, feeling that I was unlovable in my current state, drive for perfection and a need to please people. I was told from an early age that my body wasn't the "right" size or that my face was so pretty if I could just make my body match. Dieting and hating my body have been a part of my life since before I can remember. My first time on a structured weight-loss plan was when I was in middle school. My weight went up and down (but mostly up), which was another reason to try the next fad diet. *The life and the partner I wanted were just X pounds away.*

Finally, in my endless research, I found a concept called Intuitive Eating, and it started me down the path to where I am now. I realized that food wasn't the enemy, but my approach to food was actually the issue. This aha moment made me take a good look at my life and see what else needed further reflection. I found a life coach who helped me see how my past informed my present. I never fully processed my parent's divorce, the car accident, and my lack of self-worth. I saw similar patterns in my work and personal relationships and knew that I had created an environment where I couldn't live, let alone thrive. With my coach by my side, I finally had the confidence to leave the clinic I started, the identity I had adopted, and the career I thought I wanted. It was terrifying, but every step I took was in my best interest and grew my confidence in myself and my decision-making skills.

Everyone must know they are loved unconditionally, which must first come from within. This is my "why"—if I can help a woman undergoing cancer treatment make better decisions for herself and her family, without fear and with a knowledge of self, then I consider it a job well done. I know what it is like to feel that my choices are not my own or that I don't have a choice. I'm here to support my clients in their journey, be the voice that brings them back to their intuition, and help them during a very difficult time.

Share Your Brilliance

I have the ability to see things from a different perspective. As an energy healer, I believe we have not tapped into the mind's abilities. It's something that our Western medical system has not given much focus to (other than the diseased parts), and I think it's a great disservice. The mind is so powerful that, if you can believe that something is possible, you have the path to healing yourself.

When I work with clients, I help them look at all the parts of their lives that contribute to where they are now. Radical healing cannot happen unless we change the environment in which the disease takes hold. There is no shame in not knowing better, but once you do know, it is up to you to commit to the path of healing ... a coach is a great way to help with all the barriers that come up.

I offer a 360-degree view of their current health and how they can achieve their health goals. Much of that is through diet and lifestyle changes. I offer real-life tips and tricks backed by scientific evidence and thousands of years of human history.

Overcoming Challenges to Scale

My major challenge was the fear of being seen. This goes back to my dieting history and the desire not to take up space. Having an opinion about something that wasn't strictly based on guidelines can set you up for haters, particularly when it comes to cancer treatment. I knew I needed help and support, so I worked with two business coaches from the start.

I have found that even with all the growth and work I did personally before I started the business, more layers go even deeper when it's just you and the next sale. I've had to work on my relationships with money, my parents, my partner, and myself to be at a place where expressing my thoughts and opinions didn't give me an anxiety attack.

Monetizing Your Healing Gifts

I've monetized my knowledge and gifts through a consulting practice. I teach as an adjunct professor for two pharmacy schools, I work with a tech start-up building an app to connect pharmacists and patients living rurally with cancer, I work with a clinical hypnotherapist as the side effect management and nutrition expert, and I partner with a local wellness spa and herbal apothecary to provide in-person consultations. My connections through these companies bring me 1:1 clients, additional learning opportunities, and a sense of connection with the cancer community. It sounds like a lot, but many of these opportunities are seasonal or a few hours per week. I get to choose which projects I work on, which has been very freeing.

What Lights You Up About Your Business

I love seeing my clients get better, to see them go from unsure and confused to confident and thriving.

Advice Along the Journey

The hardest part is leaving the job with the salary and benefits. Going into a world of unknowns, feeling like a sleazy salesperson, and finally finding your way is hard but worth it. Entrepreneurship has its ups and downs, but I have ownership over my work and the flexibility to pivot when I need to. It is very empowering for someone who has felt disempowered most of her life.

What it Means to Be a Heart-Centered Healer in Health Care

Heart-centered care has been a game-changer in how I practice. I have always been prized for my learning, but my clients started seeing results when I started tapping into my innate knowledge as a healer, a woman, and a human. It's about connecting with people on a human level. Out of love for myself and my clients, I have learned to set healthy boundaries, but within them, I can cry and laugh in the same session with my clients. They know I will be there for them; sometimes, I may be the only one.

Trish Francetich, PharmD, RTTP, CHt is a holistic wellness coach, a practitioner of Marisa Peer's Rapid Transformational Therapy (RTT®), hypnotherapist, and pharmacist. She has over 25 years' experience in the health and wellness industry, having served in various leadership roles as a community and clinical pharmacist. Dr. Trish has been featured online in *Authority Magazine* and is a three-time summit speaker.

Dr. Trish is the CEO of Rise & Thrive Wellness LLC, where she combines her expertise in holistic wellness coaching and subconscious reprogramming with her love of leading, inspiring, and educating. She is on a mission to teach thousands of people about the power of the mind and how to build new neural pathways within the brain with hypnosis. She guides ambitious female entrepreneurs to get to the root cause of what's keeping them stuck from reaching their true potential in business, abundance, health, and relationships so they can let it go and rewire their mind to unleash their brilliance into the world.

Dr. Trish would love to connect with you! Get in touch with her through the link below where you can also download a FREE hypnosis audio to achieve unshakable confidence.

https://linktr.ee/dr.trish.francetich

Trials + Testimony into the Entrepreneurial Journey

My first personal challenge was a lengthy separation followed by divorce shortly after graduating from pharmacy school. Navigating the gamut of emotions from a failed marriage—betrayal, guilt, shame, sadness, anger, and grief—seemed at times unbearable and never ending. Three years of counseling and talk therapy taught me three things: I had codependent tendencies; I needed to be more self-reliant; and continually reliving the past was keeping me stuck and miserable. What finally helped me heal was meditation, breathwork, heart alignment with HeartMath®, Dr. Wayne Dyer's book *The Power of Intention*, and falling in love again.

The internal struggle I had throughout my 20-year career as a retail pharmacist was another challenge. I was never aligned in my job and felt like part of the healthcare problem rather than the solution. I knew I was meant to do more, be more, and create more impact. I knew I wanted to empower others to heal themselves instead of giving up and taking medications for the rest of their lives. Most of the time, I was consumed with limiting thoughts of not having a choice and feeling trapped with beliefs that I could never make as much money in another job. I abused myself with negative self-talk that left me feeling like a victim of my circumstances and unworthy of something better. I even tried convincing myself that I just needed to change my attitude while ignoring the toxic work environment.

The impetus for change was my realization that I had strayed far from my true self and my life's path. I had to get back and break the cycle of operating in survival mode. Perpetual stress had become habituated and was beginning to take a toll on my health and relationships. I hated the person I had become. I was desperate for change or I feared I would not survive another year.

With struggle comes growth, and darkness reveals light. The awakening that ensued in 2021 was discovering my "why." Something that my wise five-year old self knew, lying in the grass looking up at the stars and feeling connected to all that is: You are whole just as you are; you have all the answers inside of you; you are here to create an amazing life; and possibilities are as limitless as the sky. My "why" is to inspire others to reconnect with that knowledge and reclaim their power.

Share Your Brilliance

As an emotional empath, I am sensitive to other people's emotions. That used to leave me exhausted because I did not have the ability to differentiate my own emotions from those of the people I interacted with. Today, I see this as a gift because I feel in tune with my clients and their vision, which makes it easier to guide them and facilitate their transformation.

As a child, I loved to dance, write songs, sing, draw and make people laugh. I was full of energy. Early on, however, I learned that not everyone could handle my enthusiasm and free spirit. It got me in trouble between the ages of five and eight, which dimmed my light. I retreated within and formed the negative beliefs of "it's unsafe for me to be myself" and "I don't belong."

Many of the tools I use in my practice to facilitate healing for clients are tools I used to rid my own blocks and limiting beliefs. Rapid Transformational Therapy (RTT) and hypnotherapy are two powerful tools I use to dive deep into the subconscious mind, getting to the cause, root, and reason of limiting beliefs; letting them go for good; replacing them with new empowering beliefs more aligned with your higher purpose; and changing the trajectory of your life. It sounds like magic, but really it is based in neuroscience. The hypnosis I practice is not entertainment; it is transformational.

Overcoming Challenges to Scale

The only external factor that proved to be a challenge was my full-time pharmacist job that consumed most of my time and energy. It took about a year before I felt confident enough in the success of my business to leave my corporate job for good.

I had many internal challenges to overcome. Name a common limiting belief or block, and I had it: unworthiness, perfectionism, procrastination, fear of failure, fear of judgment, and self-sabotage, just to name a few. I worked through all of them with RTT, hypnotherapy, and 1:1 coaching.

I have had four coaches and mentors during the past year who were complete game changers for me. They helped me find clarity, crush my emotional blocks and limiting beliefs, and taught me valuable new skills on my journey to becoming an entrepreneur. Thank you, Dr. Christina Fontana, Marisa Peer, Jennifer Wheeler, and Mary Lou Rodriguez!

Monetizing Your Healing Gifts

There are many ways to work with me at varying investment levels, from online group programs to personalized 1:1 sessions via Zoom. "Zoomnosis" is indeed just as effective as hypnosis in person. The following are a list of my current offerings.

- Hypnosis audios for purchase and download on various topics.
- Group workshops and hypnosis sessions on various topics such as abundance, confidence, self-worth, sharing your gifts, habits, weight release, and more. Pre-recorded workshops will be available for purchase soon.
- Single RTT session for smoking or vaping cessation; sports, exam, and sales performance; public speaking; and more.
- Three-session RTT bundle for more complex issues (anxiety, weight release, self-sabotage).
- Five-session hypnotherapy bundle for non-regressive hypnotherapy and children.
- Signature 1:1 Hypno-Coaching for female entrepreneurs and professionals. A 16-week program that includes five RTT sessions with five coaching sessions that are highly personalized.

What Lights You Up About Your Business

Facilitating client shifts with hypnosis is my favorite part. Witnessing their transformation over the course of just a few weeks and their breakthroughs as "aha" moments during a hypnotherapy session is elating and what lights me up.

Advice Along the Journey

Moving into entrepreneurship from your current career, there are crucial facts to consider because you will be creating a new identity as a successful entrepreneur, along with new beliefs and habits.

First, you have to break the pattern of the chronic stress that you have habituated because you cannot create in survival mode. Adopting a daily ritual of healing yourself by calming your nervous system is necessary to get clear on your vision so you can take inspired action to create the outcomes you want.

Second, become aware of negative thoughts and your inner dialogue throughout the day. Stop those negative thoughts in their tracks, let them go, and tell yourself a positive thought that is more aligned with your vision.

Finally, invest in yourself, and hire a personal coach. Better yet, hire a coach who is also a hypnotherapist! It will significantly accelerate the transition to entrepreneurship because, as my mentor Mary Lou Rodriguez says, "Hypnosis is the rocket fuel for transformation."

What it Means to Be a Heart-Centered Healer in Health Care

Being a heart-centered health care practitioner means being real and serving with love. Because everything we crave—whether it is peace, joy, freedom, belonging or love—is on the other side of service. It is about being devoted to making an impact, feeling connected, in the flow, and aligned. It is about wanting all that and more for my clients. It is always about holding my clients' vision of what they want to believe about themselves, who they want to be, and how they want to show up in the world. Guiding them to tap into their innate power to heal at the subconscious level, make breakthroughs, and see their vision become reality—that brings me joy and validation that I am fulfilling my life's purpose.

Angela Orr, RPh is a stress and health management coach. She is a certified HeartMath practitioner, certified Stress and Well Being Assessment provider, executive coach, and pharmacist of 37 years.

As a serial entrepreneur, Angela has had many businesses, including owning and operating two independent pharmacies for 15 years in Maine.

She decided to go on a healing journey after a breast cancer diagnosis and realizing stress was killing her. On this journey, she explored modalities around physical and mental health. Angela found several that she believes helped save her life.

She then courageously sold her pharmacies and pivoted into coaching and mentoring to share her knowledge. Her specialty is using the HeartMath techniques and technology to help clients heal at an epigenetic level.

She has also developed employee/team stress and health management programs. Her clients are primarily healthcare organizations, hospice organizations, and independent pharmacies.

Trials + Testimony into the Entrepreneurial Journey

I will never forget that day. The phone call. The diagnosis. Yes, the biopsy came back, and it is positive. You have breast cancer.

Here I was a business owner of two pharmacies with lots of friends, networks of colleagues, many family activities, and travel. From the outside looking in, it seemed that I had it all and was so happy and successful.

This led me to really stop and look at my life. Stress was literally killing me. Killing me! I was now a breast cancer patient, functional alcoholic, morbidly obese, and truly a very unhappy, stressed out, and worry-holic woman.

I had overcome so much. I was born into a very dysfunctional family: alcoholic father, prescription-addicted mother, and many issues in the extended family.

My family was very poor—never had a new car, a home of our own. We lived in government subsidized housing, or as we called it "the projects"! We didn't have the newest or greatest gadgets, clothes, or items other kids had. Sometimes we didn't even have a working bathroom in our home. That's for another day.

I have since come to terms with my childhood. As I like to say, it is never too late to have a happy childhood. My parents did the best they could, and I am grateful to them. Without all of these experiences I would not be who I am and where I am, and I like where I am in life.

I was the first person in my extended family to graduate college. And a pharmacist at that! Since then my siblings have all gone on to higher education, and two are nurses, one is a physical therapist, and one is a master's-educated educator. I would say we all made it out of the ghetto!

Not only was my home-life rough; public life growing up was no picnic either. I was teased, taunted, and bullied—either about my poor family, my eccentric style, or my weight. Even my high school guidance counselor refused to help me apply for college. He laughed at me and said I would never make it from the wrong side of the tracks! Thank God another counselor helped me. One thing I always had was my intelligence. Doing well in school helped me move ahead in life.

When I was in high school, I remember thinking, "One day I will be rich and will show you!" Going to pharmacy school was my answer to making a lot of money. Looking back now, I also believe it was a way for me to help the world. Being a natural-born healer, I see now that it's important to me to make a positive contribution to the world.

I have always been a serial entrepreneur, so I could have time and money freedom. This led me to the journey of pharmacy ownership. I loved being a pharmacy owner; however, I knew that with the turn in my health, I needed to re-evaluate everything in my life. It was great news that my surgeon told me I was an "uninteresting case"—a simple surgery with a high likelihood of return to health.

After successful treatment, I began on my healing journey. I knew I could not live life the same as before the diagnosis.

Share Your Brilliance

Because I could not continue life as I had been living before my breast cancer diagnosis, I thought about how I could go forward and what needs to change. In managing my stress and well-being, I have stopped alcohol use, lost a significant amount of weight, and am happier and more at peace then I have ever been.

I am a natural-born healer and a very compassionate, caring person who has so much empathy for others. With this softness, I also bring intuition to guide others to see things in themselves they would otherwise not be aware of.

I use various tools, such as meditation, HeartMath tools, EFT/TFT (tapping techniques), journaling, and breathing techniques to help my clients transform. This helps them see life differently and shift their internal state of being. I help them gain a heart-centered approach to living. This helps them reduce stress and internal chaos so they can live in joy and peace no matter what is going on around them.

My clients have so many results, such as decreasing or stopping medications or not needing to start them, better sleep, decreased stress and anxiety, mental clarity, decreased fatigue, weight loss, more confidence, and emotional balance to name a few!

Overcoming Challenges to Scale

The biggest challenge was to overcome myself and my self-doubts. Although I have accomplished so much in life, I didn't think I was good enough and wondered, "Who am I to say I could help people in this way?"

By continuing to work on myself, I have overcome my own internal limitations. Wellness is a journey for me, not a destination.

Externally, this showed up for me as not wanting to expose myself or my weaknesses because I didn't want others to think I was bad or weak. I have also had some friends and family not believe in what I am doing. They just don't understand why I don't want to continue being a pharmacist, which is a "good, safe job"! Again, as I have grown and healed, I realize I don't need everyone's blessing. I stay focused on who I can help and who wants that help.

Monetizing Your Healing Gifts

In the past, my gifts have helped me become a successful multi-pharmacy owner. Currently, I offer several programs, ranging from one-on-one sessions. to group sessions for stress and well-being management and exclusive women's retreats.

I have programs for employers and healthcare institutions. I am excited to also be introducing a program for independent pharmacies to offer their patients.

What Lights You Up About Your Business

I love seeing my clients be able to self-regulate emotionally. To be able to go through stress and not be triggered into past feelings, emotions, or behaviors.

I love seeing them work with their doctor and have medications de-prescribed because they don't need them any longer.

I love to hear them laugh, enjoy their life, and have fun. It is so rewarding to have someone say to me, "I really enjoyed my family tonight instead of just wanting to have that glass of wine or piece of cake when I got home from work."

Their stress is so reduced that they don't want to escape from life any longer. They can finally enjoy the moment and be present for their life.

Advice Along the Journey

Invest in yourself and hire a coach. It is very hard to be objective about your gifts and talents, especially in the beginning of your entrepreneur journey. Be aware of and present in your journey—life it is not a straight line from A to B. Have fun along the way!

Take action no matter how small it may seem. I like to say that imperfect action trumps perfect inaction every single time!

What it Means to Be a Heart-Centered Healer in Health Care

It is about being a leader in the new world of healthcare. Not to view people as "patients" but as those who need and want to feel whole and complete. I also believe that primary care should be about preventing disease. In prevention, we can avoid chronic diseases and throwing a pill at every problem.

Dr. Katie Wood is a mother, pharmacist, and integrative nutrition health coach specializing in fertility and women's health. She is the founder of Pharm to Wellness LLC and the brand Happy Nourished Motherhood. Dr. Katie helps women over 30 nourish their mind & body for optimal fertility health so they can confidently conceive with ease.

Dr. Katie comes with eight years of experience as a retail pharmacist; this background in conventional medicine is what first piqued her awareness that people need more intimate coaching toward health and vitality without depending on pharmaceuticals. After experiencing a lack of support and education through her fertility and pregnancy journey, she became determined to advocate for women's health. Dr. Katie is passionate about supporting and empowering women on their fertility and pregnancy, transitioning into motherhood, using her calm, gentle guidance and taking a holistic approach focusing on nutrition, lifestyle, and self-care.

You can find out more at www.happynourishedmotherhood.com.

Trials + Testimony into the Entrepreneurial Journey

When my husband and I decided it was time to expand our family, I had been on oral contraceptives for over 13 years. Feeling nervous yet optimistic, I discontinued my birth control the same month we started trying to conceive, under the guidance of my OB-GYN. Little did I realize, even as a pharmacist, the damage that hormonal contraceptives can have on your body and the amount of healing that needs to take place post-pill.

I consulted my provider on three different occasions regarding my fertility and was never given any advice, support, or actionable steps. I was always told, "everything looks normal," and to keep trying. Eventually, they recommended that I schedule an appointment with a fertility specialist at the one-year mark without an offer to run labs or discuss nutrition or lifestyle changes to support healthy fertility.

After seven months of negative pregnancy tests, frustration, and desperation I decided to try alternative medicine. It wasn't until then that I truly realized the toll that hormonal birth control took on my body. With the guidance of my acupuncturist, I used Chinese herbal medicine, acupuncture, whole foods, and practical ways to support and heal my body.

Three months later, I fell pregnant with our beautiful daughter, Olivia. Reflecting on my 10 months of fertility struggles, I realized the loss of connection and knowledge that women have with their bodies, and the lack of support in the conventional space. As a coach, I've witnessed the imprudent recommendation for women to medicate their bodies to force ovulation before treating the root cause to allow the body to heal with nutrition and lifestyle changes.

All this to say, because of my journey to and in the thick of motherhood, along with eight years of retail pharmacist experience, I started noticing more and more flaws in our medical system. I became a pharmacist to educate patients and make a positive impact in their lives. As the years went on as a pharmacist, it became apparent that the reality of doing the work I was being pulled to do in my current space was a mirage in the distance. Retail pharmacy simply does not support the type of personalized patient-centered care I wanted to give.

Share Your Brilliance

As I have become more connected with myself and attuned with my unique gifts, I have learned that I am a good listener, deeply empathetic, and intuitive, and I have a keen sense of people's energies. People want to feel seen and heard, and that is one way that I support my clients—by being present with them, listening to their concerns and struggles without judgment. When working with me, my clients are wrapped in a warm and nurturing container, with gentle love and guidance. I have been told on many occasions that I emanate calmness, peace, and even-keeled energy.

Going through my fertility struggles, I had to learn how to be patient, surrender to divine timing and trust in my body's ability to heal. In my journey through motherhood, I realized how vital it is for us women to feel comfortable with voicing our needs. Our society of instant gratification and conventional medicine's "my way or the highway" ideal has caused a shift where some women have lost their voice. My desire is to help women confidently feel liberated in their feminine power, express their needs, and advocate for their health.

I share any useful tools that I've learned along the way or healing gifts that I've tapped into with my clients. This includes meditation, breathwork, journaling, visualization, tapping, and Eden Energy Medicine.

Overcoming Challenges to Scale

One big challenge to starting my business was the idea of stepping away from the security of a full-time job. This highlighted an internal block of mine, which is fear of failure and feeling not good/smart enough to succeed. I experienced money blocks such as fear of not having any or enough and that it won't stick around. At some point, I needed to make the decision that my degree does not define me or shackle me to a classical pharmacist role. The next challenge was what I could do with my PharmD. Do I need another certification or degree? I enrolled at the Institute for Integrative Nutrition, and once I received my health coaching certification, other blocks came up as I set the foundation for my business—imposter syndrome, fear of being seen or liked on social media, and the dreaded "compare and despair."

If it wasn't for working with Christina, I don't know where I would be. I have known Christina for over a year now, and looking back to where I was, I am in awe of how far I've come in terms of personal and business development. Beginning with her self-paced courses and meditations, I finally understood what a "block" was and accepted that I have some! I'm grateful that I've been able to attend two of her transformative retreats, and the energy after the second one was so impactful that I immediately signed up to work 1:1 with her. The work I am doing with Christina is life changing, and I am blessed to have her love, support, and guidance along the way.

Monetizing Your Healing Gifts

I first monetized my gifts with 1:1 coaching, and I absolutely love offering this intimate container. However, to show up fully for my clients and to be present with my family, I began group coaching and memberships so I can expand and reach more women, while respecting my boundaries and needs. I offer a high-value PDF on strategies for a healthy fertility, mediation bundles, an exclusive membership and personal essential oil rollers. For free content, I have a private Facebook group where I share value and support my members as well as a blog on my website.

What Lights You Up About Your Business

One of my favorite parts when working retail in a smaller community was the connection and relationship I built with my patients, so it's no surprise that I love this part about working closely with my clients! We have a mutual trust and become weaved into each other's lives, in a sense, because we get to know each other outside of coaching. When I get to help facilitate lifelong positive changes, I like to think that our time together is something they cherish and carry with them as well. Making healthier changes and being committed can be a challenge for some, so when I hear that one of my clients has a big win, whether it's feeling energized, regulating their cycle or a positive pregnancy test, my heart bursts with love and excitement for them. Coaching women to bring forth health and vitality into their lives, whether it's for overall well-being or to nourish themselves and their future children, truly fills my cup and brings hope for future generations.

Advice Along the Journey

My first piece of advice is to dial into what truly lights you up and brings you joy. Be clear on what your "why" is and who you want to serve. My second piece of advice is to surrender, trust, and invest in yourself! You must surrender to the process and understand that great things take time. Trust in your unique gifts and intuition. Always remember that investing in yourself and your dreams is worth it, and that it's safe to ask for help!

What it Means to Be a Heart-Centered Healer in Health Care

Being a heart-centered practitioner means you're sharing your innate and unique gifts with the world. When it comes from the heart, that type of energy is expansive and potent.

Dr. Elisabeth Wygant is a women's hormone and gut health guru, functional nutrition expert, contributor to *Best Holistic Life Magazine*, speaker, host of the Thrive Mama! Podcast, wife, and mother of two little ladies. Her specialty is empowering ambitious women who are feeling overwhelmed, fatigued, and short on time to move in confidence, reclaim their libido, and optimize energy levels. She emboldens women to unearth their feminine superpower through deep inner healing via embodiment techniques, cycle syncing, and more!

Her true passion in life is inspiring women to fill their cup and recognize that it is never too late to invest in themselves and their health!

Hey girl, hey! Let's connect, join me on LinkedIn: https://www.linkedin.com/in/drelisabethwygant/

Check out my FREE Hormone Personality Quiz to learn more about possible hormonal imbalances going on in that beautiful bod of yours! https://bit.ly/HormonePersonalityQuiz

Trials + Testimony into the Entrepreneurial Journey

My entire journey in this life has brought me to my purpose. To claim that these events haven't come with challenges would be a lie. Yet, what doesn't challenge you doesn't change you.

I began my career as a traditional community pharmacist, and I was in the thick of hustle culture. I was on the war path to create the American Dream!

However, in the midst of all of this came a sense of turmoil within me. I realized almost immediately after starting my career that I was unfulfilled. I witnessed drug abuse, prescriber abuse, and dependency so heavily on medications as if somehow taking a medication would be the saving grace for ALL health conditions. It was a heavy load to carry and I tried to convince myself that this was just "part of the job."

Then, I became a mother, and that changed everything!

With my first pregnancy I experienced a traumatic delivery. It involved a failed epidural, a severe spinal headache, my pain that was caused by the epidural being ignored, and a vacuum extraction. Due to the failed epidural I wasn't able to hold and nurture my newborn daughter the way I had envisioned, and it was heartbreaking! I felt detached from her and as though I was an unworthy mother. I developed postpartum anxiety and postpartum depression shortly after giving birth. It took the support of my husband, my best friend, and family to nurture both my baby and myself to be lifted out of this very heavy space. It takes a village to raise a child, but it ALSO takes one to support a mother.

When I became pregnant with my second, I decided that, this go around, I wanted a non-medicated birth. I did it, and I felt like a QUEEN! Yet, shortly after coming home from the hospital, she developed a fever at only 10 days old. We were admitted to the pediatric ICU for several days. There, we waited with angst. All we could do was pray and allow the providers to help heal our baby. Thankfully she pulled through, and she is thriving to this day!

After my pregnancies, I made the decision to breastfeed both of my daughters, and I felt so much pressure to do it all. By "do it all," I mean at the same time—to carry out my role as the pharmacist and eat all while pumping! I was so scared that if I spoke up about my working conditions I would be let go. For me that looked like being buried by student loan debt, being a new mother, and scrambling to find a new pharmacist position in a rural community. This is the reality that so many women face: choosing between family or career and being terrified of losing their job because they are making decisions that are best for their family. It's truly heartbreaking that the life forces of the world are treated in such a way!

Soon after returning to work after my second little was born, I became severely ill with mastitis that landed me in the hospital. Then, I had the epiphany that my experiences in my career and motherhood were not uniquely my own. I knew that the life forces of this world endured this pain to a lesser or greater extent. It was then I uncovered my purpose!

I know that for my girls and all women to THRIVE, I must change the world! Thus, Elisabeth Wygant Wellness was born. My purpose is to empower, enlighten, and educate women that they are worthy of unleashing their feminine superpowers that our world is craving!

Share Your Brilliance

There's unrest and chaos taking over our world, and it's time for women to awaken and rise.

To do so, we must focus on self, nurture our feminine wisdom that's within, and step away from cultural norms. We must reunite with the inner self that has been waiting to be freed so we can balance the masculine energy that has suppressed and destroyed many with the feminine energy that will unite and create harmony.

Guiding my clients through this transformational process of reigniting their femininity is unlike any other shift I've ever witnessed. Together we build the foundation of embracing and embodying the woman that's been hiding deep within the womb through guided meditations, alongside nourishing her body with nutrition that realigns hormones during each phase of her cycle (even if she is pregnant or transitioning into menopause). In doing so, she reconnects to her inner wisdom and is able to step into her power!

Overcoming Challenges to Scale

I had a major internal block surrounding speaking my truth! I was scared to step up and out on my platform because I was scared of how I would be viewed by my community. However, once I did, it was one of the most empowering moments of my life! I realized my story and my voice need to be heard because together we will positively affect change.

These blocks have taken a lot of inner work and investing in myself to move through. Of course I'm still a masterpiece in the making, as we all are, and am always in the healing process. It took investing in business coaches who not only guided me in strategy, but also in personal growth. It's been such a blessing to work with Rebecca Cafiero, Dr. Melissa Henault, Jana Short, and Kelly Roach! Without their guidance, I don't know where I would be today. From the bottom of my heart, thank you!

Monetizing Your Healing Gifts

There are literally limitless possibilities to monetize your capabilities and healing powers beyond what you're doing today! That's what makes entrepreneurship so exciting!

I have found that having a tiered approach for working with clients is super helpful because that way you can have touch points utilizing your healing modalities. I personally have a low-ticket offer for a Hormonal Harmony Toolkit, several courses that are self-paced, a group program, and one-on-one offers. I'm currently in the process of launching a beta corporate wellness initiative. See what I mean by limitless possibilities?

What Lights You Up About Your Business

The transformation that I witness even within the first week of working with my clients is off the charts! I get so hyped up for my clients when they have breakthroughs and show up on camera in this confident goddess glow. I truly love being a guide in such a powerful transition in women's lives!

Advice Along the Journey

Stop. Breathe. Listen.

Give yourself space to hear what your soul is speaking to you. Step out of the hustle and just sit in silence. You're deserving of this, sister! When fear begins to creep in and stomp on your dreams, acknowledge it, and recognize that it's there to protect you. Release this fear, give it a squeeze, and breathe it out Replace that fear with faith in yourself. You've done hard work before, right? (For example, pharmacy school and your career.) But what if this dream you have for yourself is the stepping stone to your happiness and freedom?

When the world begins to crack open, it's a chance for you to seek the opportunity that's unfolding. Bet on you, girlfriend, you can't go wrong!

What it Means to Be a Heart-Centered Healer in Health Care

To me, being a heart-centered healer in healthcare is the premise of embarking on the journey of patient and/or client care. It's recognizing that we are all human and what we truly crave is compassion and unity. To also be heard and understood when it comes to wellbeing. I sincerely believe that when you are considered a "healer," you look at the person as a whole in mind, body, and spirit.

Dr. Mariam Yanikyan is a holistic pharmacist and a self-love and empowerment coach helping women prioritize themselves and their health. She was a retail pharmacist for over 13 years. In July of 2020, she made the decision to quit retail pharmacy and pursue her dream of becoming a heart-centered entrepreneur. She is the founder of Self

Love First LLC, nurturing a mindset and lifestyle transformation that begins as soon as you put YOURSELF FIRST and reach for the highest and truest version of yourself.

Her clients are new moms, high-achieving career women, and other former pharmacists who have put their health first and started to follow their heart's dreams and desires. This entrepreneurial journey is also a spiritual awakening for her, challenging her every step of the way to face her fears and overcome them with courage. You can reach her through her website at www.mySelfLoveFirst.com.

Trials + Testimony into the Entrepreneurial Journey

The biggest challenge I faced that started me on this entrepreneurial journey was my desire to heal from the trauma of my past. I wanted to know how to face emotions of guilt, shame, and fear of my past trauma and become the healthiest, most empowered version of myself. Once I saw how empowering this process was, I got inspired to teach it and share it in my own way. I realized self-love was the key that opened the doors to my heart and my highest self, hence my coaching company's name, "Self Love First LLC." I am passionate about the power of self-love and self-empowerment to transform women's lives—healing through our emotions by putting ourselves, our mental/emotional health, first.

Share Your Brilliance

The short answer to this question for me is self-love. Self-love is my superpower. It is the driving force behind my courage to be vulnerable with myself, and with others by sharing my story. I have dealt with childhood abandonment, separation, and sexual abuse through most of my teenage years. I am a recovering people pleaser. I am highly intuitive and empathic. I am powerful, passionate, and dedicated to living as the most authentic version of myself. I wear my soul on my sleeves. My most important tools are self-love and self-compassion. This is also what I teach my clients: worthiness, trust, and love in themselves. I also teach about balancing our divine feminine and masculine energy to birth our dreams and desires into reality. I teach how to connect to one's heart through guided meditation. I empower my clients to be vulnerable through radical self-expression and other tools (i.e. EFT [Emotional Freedom Technique], breath work) to help move the energy of our emotions. I am a healer in that I see the highest version of my clients and can hold the space necessary for them to see and believe it too. I believe in the energy of love, forgiveness, compassion, and kindness of SELF to heal, restore, and rejuvenate all pain and trauma.

Overcoming Challenges to Scale

There were many internal challenges or blocks to overcome at every level of growing my business. Even though I was a seasoned retail pharmacist and health coaching was part of the job, I was never entrepreneurial or business-minded. I felt all the fears of failure, of success, of not being good enough, and not feeling worthy of my dreams. Taking consistent action in my business is still one of my struggles today. What helped enormously to push the ball forward was investing in the coaching programs my mentors were offering. I did not know the first thing about growing an online coaching business, so I needed all the help I could get. Getting support at every level of my business is still a crucial and ongoing process. I had to overcome the perfectionist in me that wanted to do it all alone. I no longer feel like an imposter at what I do, yet I still hold some fear of being seen or heard. I crave sharing my story and empowering women through it. I had to let go of self-judgment, perfectionism, and my people pleasing tendencies to keep showing up in a bigger way. I let go of the skeptics, and surrounded myself with people who loved and supported me and my vision. Even the closest people in my life had and still have doubts about my choice to open my own coaching business. Yet it has not stopped me. I will keep growing.

Monetizing Your Healing Gifts

I would like to admit "monetizing your healing gifts" brought up so much resistance in me at the beginning. It took a while to realize the value of the energetic exchange once my clients committed to paying for my services.

I have created a Self-love Meditation Bundle that includes five quick and easy ways to connect to your heart, ground your energy, and start the day with high vibes.

I also do yearly Self Love Retreats and online "Feel to Heal" Workshops that include meditation, radical self-expression, and EFT.

I am currently working on creating a membership portal called Divine Feminine Queen, where members will have monthly group calls, PDFs, videos, and guided meditations to embody their Queen essence and amplify their self-worth.

My Self-love Healing Sessions involve personalized 1:1 coaching plus a guided energy cleansing meditation that dives deep into the subconscious resistance and reprograms it to higher frequencies of self-love and worthiness. These sessions are very powerful, and never the same. I recommend at least six sessions, but clients feel the change in their energy from the first session.

What Lights You Up About Your Business

This may be selfish to admit (or self-loving), but every time a new client signs up for my coaching programs, I get a rush of gratitude and confirmation that I am following my dreams and someone out there needs my gifts. I get the same feeling when they write a testimonial of how their life was changed due to our work together. I also get this feeling in women's retreats. I have been to two of Christina's Elevate Retreats and have transformed and taken huge leaps forward in my business because of them. I hosted my own local retreat last year in celebration of the one-year anniversary of Self Love First. Hosting retreats is a dream that continues to grow and take shape for me. Something powerful happens when like-minded women come together with common intentions to heal, to release, to grow, and to transform. Our energy gets amplified and shifts in consciousness happen quickly in such loving and supportive spaces. Self Love First's second retreat will happen later this year.

Advice Along the Journey

The biggest piece of advice I would give is for entrepreneurs to INVEST in themselves and their vision. It is not a one-time-only investment. The quicker you come to terms with investing in yourself continuously for personal development, the quicker you will grow. It is really that simple. Invest even if you don't believe in yourself or your business. Feeling unworthy is the biggest block in this type of healing practice.

The next thing is to surround yourself with people on similar paths. This means letting go of those people who are not supportive and put you or your ideas down. Take the pressure of explaining it to them off yourself. They are just not where you are right now, and that's ok. Let go of judgment. Surround yourself with people, places, and spaces that are supportive. Allowing SUPPORT in is huge. Know you are always supported divinely when you follow your heart, your dreams, your desires. Allow yourself to be guided to the right support for you (i.e. hiring a coach, a VA, etc.).

What it Means to Be a Heart-Centered Healer in Healthcare

It means you pour your heart and soul into your practice. It means setting and following your own rules and boundaries based on your needs and desires. It means freedom to create through your healing business using your intuition, allowing divine guidance to come through. To me it means incorporating the divine feminine energy along with the masculine energy to create from the heart.

Personalized Medicine

Dr. Jennifer Marquez is married to Michael and is a mother to Tessa. They live in Hamilton, Ga., with their miniature schnauzer, Sassy.

Dr. Jennifer earned her PharmD from Auburn University Harrison College of Pharmacy and then completed a PGY-1 pharmacy practice residency. She has practiced in progressive roles in an ambulatory care medication assistance clinic, anticoagulation clinic, and a medical oncology clinic. She is board certified in oncology and also has a certification in pharmacogenomics (PGx).

In 2021, Dr. Jennifer founded her business PharmDNA, LLC, which provides PGx and medication consulting services both directly to patients as well as to healthcare providers. She is a member of several organizations that are committed to advancing the implementation of PGx for the benefit of patients. Her passion is using her knowledge and gifts to make her greatest contribution to patient care through her business.

You can connect with her on LinkedIn at https://www.linkedin.com/in/drjennifermarquez.

Trials + Testimony into the Entrepreneurial Journey

I personally know what it is like to face death. My own brush with death, and my related journey in grief from losing my triplet children (Cassidy, Camden, and Canaan) in 2012, has shaped my entire outlook on life, purpose, passion, what I complain about, and how I spend my time.

These experiences, paired with my extensive experience working in oncology, have permanently imprinted my mind with thoughts about the brevity of life and my need to be intentional with my time and my actions, not only personally but in my career.

The beautiful story about how my heart healed, how I met my husband Michael, and how our daughter Tessa came into our lives changed the trajectory and the purpose of my life forever. I want to use my skills and talents as a pharmacist in the highest possible contribution that I can make to my God, my family, my friends, my patients, and myself. I want nothing more than to make them all proud.

Share Your Brilliance

I'm a problem-solver—I embrace a challenge! My area of practice is in pharmacogenomics (PGx), which is the study of how your DNA influences your response to drug therapy. The complexities of medicine, genetics, lifestyle factors, and their interplay are fascinating and provide endless opportunities for me to expand, learn, and shine in my role as a pharmacist. If I'm being completely transparent, I also love doing difficult things (especially if someone says it cannot be done)!

I'm obviously biased, but pharmacists are brilliant. In many situations, they are neither valued nor appreciated. I want to practice at the top of my degree! I want to live a life of my own design, not fulfilling someone else's plans and dreams. I figured out that my own dreams are urgent and that no one else is going to pursue them for me! It is MY responsibility to go hard after my dreams ... so I am.

I thoroughly enjoy educating and bringing awareness to the public about my field. Creating social media content related to PGx is a wonderful outlet for me—a very fulfilling and fun part of what I do. I enjoy using my quick wit and keen sense of humor to make my points. I thrive on making the complicated premises of PGx understandable for everyone.

Overcoming Challenges to Scale

Challenges during my entrepreneurial journey have included feeling inadequate, fear of failure, financial strains, time constraints from working a job and running a business, relationship strains, learning to say no, perfectionism, putting myself in the public eye, and doing things while afraid.

I have become very comfortable being uncomfortable! I have learned that planning is wonderful, but acting is the important part that must follow planning.

Did I eagerly seek out public speaking and instantly feel comfortable putting myself in the public eye? No. But did I do it anyway? Absolutely—because my dreams are urgent, and my dreams are bigger and more important to me than my fear of failure.

Most people that have regrets have them about things they DIDN'T DO. It really is better to try and fail than to never try at all. The fears that we don't face become our limitations.

Monetizing Your Healing Gifts

I started my business in PGx consulting and comprehensive medication management to provide consults directly to patients. I created a social media content site with a fellow PGx pharmacist, with the aim of helping other pharmacists who are trying to launch and market their businesses. I also do PGx consults and chronic care management (CCM) services collaboratively with a physician practice. I became an affiliate partner with a dietary supplement brand that I trust and use personally.

I never dreamed there were so many ways that I could monetize my skills and knowledge as a pharmacist. If you have the passion and the idea, you can do it!

What Lights You Up About Your Business

I love PGx! I love reading about it, talking about it, even joking about it! While it can be a complicated and intimidating field to discuss, I thrive on discussing its benefits with everyone and making it understandable for them. People are always excited to learn that your genetics can affect your medications, and they like talking about it! I also love the sense of relief and validation that many patients feel when they find out that their genetics likely contributed to medication issues they've experienced in the past.

I have a passion for networking. People are fascinating! The connections I have made in one short year in my new field have been mind-blowing. I have connected with people from all over the world and learned about their cultures, I have learned about new opportunities, companies, and fields of work.

One of the best things you can do for yourself is to network. It takes practice, but anyone can do it! Don't be afraid to show your passion, your personality, your heart. You do not simply equal what you do for a living. People really don't care what you know until they know that you care. Show people how amazing you are—all of you! Genuinely invest yourself in interacting with others' posts. Be engaging, interesting, funny—just be real. The more you share and interact, the more others will share and interact with you. This is the beauty of social networking, and it can be magic for you and your business. I have been overwhelmed with the people who have told me that I've inspired and motivated them by my posts. You can make much more of an impact than you ever dreamed possible.

I thrive on laughter. It really does wonders for your soul. I like to keep my social media posts balanced by posting a combination of silly, lighthearted, inspirational, educational, personal, and scientific content. People connect with you more deeply when you show them more of your personality and heart. I enjoy those deeper connections. Many of my professional connections have become dear friends.

Advice Along the Journey

If you want to grow, personally or professionally, you must network—and you must do it intentionally. Connect with people who are doing innovative things in your field. Interact in a meaningful and thoughtful way with their social media posts. Seek to add value to them and support them before you ask anyone for anything for yourself. Be genuine and authentic.

Put yourself out there and be bold—they're going to love you just like you are! Find people you admire and trust—connect with them. Read what they read. Learn from them. Then do what you learn!

What it Means to Be a Heart-Centered Healer in Health Care

I strive to live a life of integrity, doing the right thing for the right reasons, even if no one is watching. In healthcare, we are meeting people when they are most vulnerable and raw. Many times, you might meet them on the worst day of their lives. This is not something to be taken lightly and I believe there is an undeniable responsibility for healthcare providers to practice ethically. The best healthcare providers do what is right, for the right reasons, and they invest their heart in it. Everyone wins—the patient, caregiver, and healthcare provider.

All too often, however, the great pressures and busyness that come along with being in a healthcare-related field keep us too busy to genuinely practice heart-centered care. It is my hope that, through my business, I can truly practice at the top of my degree and feel deeply fulfilled as I meet the needs of others in meaningful ways.

Functional Medicine

Dr. Lauren Castle is the founder of the Functional Medicine Pharmacists Alliance (www.FMPhA.org), the first association representing pharmacists in functional medicine. FMPhA supports members practicing functional medicine across all pharmacy settings by uniting leaders in the field to provide continuing education, training, networking, events, and advocacy.

Dr. Lauren also serves as a functional medicine consultant pharmacist with the PharmToTable Team and maintains a part-time practice as a retail pharmacist. She received her doctor of pharmacy from Ohio Northern University in 2013 and her master of science in human nutrition and functional medicine from the University of Western States in 2018. Lauren has also studied with the Institute for Functional Medicine and Functional Medicine University, and in 2022, she became an Applied Functional Medicine Certified (AFMC) practitioner through the School of Applied Functional Medicine.

To download a free Functional Medicine Pharmacist Checklist, visit www.FMPhA.org/newsletter today.

Trials + Testimony into the Entrepreneurial Journey

I've had an interest in entrepreneurship ever since I started working at an independent pharmacy in high school. Through college, I was certain that I'd graduate and become an owner. But I ended up meeting my husband, getting a new internship with a mass retail pharmacy, and staying on with them for the next 11 years. But this path is also what led me to discover my true passion: functional medicine.

In 2015, my husband was facing numerous health issues. One day, I got a flier on our doorstep about a place called Integrative Wellness Centers with a whole list of symptoms that matched his. He went to a seminar that weekend, learned all about this concept of functional medicine, and enrolled in a 12-week program. They did extensive testing and discovered that he had gluten and dairy sensitivities, low vitamin D, early insulin resistance, and candida. We eliminated the foods causing the inflammation, treated the overgrowth, and replenished his nutrient needs. His symptoms went away, and that's when I knew that functional medicine was truly the future of healthcare.

Share Your Brilliance

I set out to learn more about functional medicine, which led me to pursue my master's degree in human nutrition and functional medicine from the University of Western States. I began helping my own patients as a retail pharmacy manager in Flint, Mich., during the height of the Flint Water Crisis when so many were struggling with lead toxicity. I integrated a functional medicine approach with traditional pharmacy services into something I called Functional Medication Therapy Management™.

But beyond serving my patients in this new way, I also wanted to help other pharmacists learn about this life-changing practice. In 2017, I began lecturing on functional medicine at state association meetings and national webinars and started a Facebook group to connect like-minded pharmacists. By that summer, I decided to create a website for pharmacists like me who were searching for answers. Thus, the Functional Medicine Pharmacists Alliance was born.

Overcoming Challenges to Scale

When I first started sharing my functional medicine knowledge in 2017, I wasn't even thinking about creating a business. I was happily employed and recently promoted to a clinical pharmacist role. I enjoyed sharing my knowledge freely. In 2018, we had our first in-person meetup at the pharmacy symposium. I was also promoted again to a market director at work, which had been my dream job since my intern days.

In 2019, our FMPhA Facebook group reached over 500 members. At our second in-person meetup, someone asked me how they could pay dues to become an FMPhA member, and I said, "There are no dues. It's *just* a Facebook group."

That is when the wise Jerrica Dodd told me, "*You better monetize this thing!*" I struggled with the idea of "*Who am I to create a pharmacy organization?*" and "*Why would anyone want to pay to join, especially when there is a free Facebook group that's now 1,500 members strong?*"

Just two weeks after the symposium, Jerrica introduced me to Danielle Perrodin, who became my life and style coach to help me step into my executive presence for a special assignment: to pitch my dream of creating a healthy food cafe and functional medicine clinic for my employer. It was the opportunity of a lifetime, but when the project ended abruptly 90 days later, I realized then that I couldn't rely on others to make my vision of bringing functional medicine into the mainstream a reality. That's when I officially took the leap into entrepreneurship and formed FMPhA, LLC, in January 2020.

Little did I know, the real challenges were just about to begin. We hit a global pandemic that changed pharmacy as we knew it. I became a caregiver for my mom, who fought liver cirrhosis and bipolar disorder before her passing at the age of 59. I faced my own battle with anxiety, depression, and burnout from trying to do it all, forcing me to take a 10-week leave from work. I ended up stepping down from my market director position and accepting a remote role where I could hone my skills in social media marketing while continuing to grow FMPhA.

The last five years since beginning FMPhA haven't been easy, but through all the ups and downs, my husband Seth has truly been my biggest supporter who has helped me overcome any challenge that came my way. Without him, I may never have discovered functional medicine or created FMPhA.

Monetizing Your Healing Gifts

I realized that my gifts were truly in creating community and collaborating with others to help pharmacists on their first steps into functional medicine. I sought to make functional medicine as accessible and affordable as possible. Our first partnership was with the Institute for Functional Medicine (IFM). We created a winning opportunity for all: a joint membership so pharmacists could have access to discounted rates for functional medicine training, while we increased the representation of pharmacist members in IFM and provided our first dues to support the work of FMPhA. We've continued to add more value to the FMPhA membership each year.

What Lights You Up About Your Business

I light up whenever I meet a pharmacist who is just beginning their functional medicine journey and they have discovered FMPhA. They feel like they have found the answers they were searching for. I've invested over $40,000 into seven years of research to truly understand this space and carve out a role for pharmacists. To then be able to help someone else fast-track their path, find joy in their profession again, and be able to positively transform their patients' lives through the lens of functional medicine is the most rewarding feeling.

Advice Along the Journey

When I first decided to shift FMPhA from a Facebook group into a business, I thought I needed to incorporate as a nonprofit organization. But I learned about the concept of creating a "heart-centered business" through Marie Forleo. Essentially, when you are considering a move into entrepreneurship, you must ask yourself why. Entrepreneurship is not without risk and hard work, so your motivation must be something so powerful that it keeps you going, no matter what. For me, my "why" is because I want to change the world for the better.

What it Means to Be a Heart-Centered Healer in Health Care

For many, becoming a healthcare practitioner comes from a place of wanting to serve and help others. I know this was true for me. While the profession of pharmacy has changed and many feel jaded, tapping into our heart to truly see our patients or clients for who they are is the only way to create a therapeutic partnership where healing can occur. This is why I feel so strongly about the functional medicine approach; it recognizes that we are complex beings and that health is not merely the absence of disease, but a positive vitality that comes from experiencing optimal alignment of the body, mind, and spirit. It is an honor and a privilege to be that trusted guide for someone on their healing journey; to be a heart-centered practitioner in healthcare.

Lauren's chapter is written in loving memory of her mom,

Peggy Snell-Anderson

November 10, 1961 – September 12, 2021

Dr. Angela Cates is a pharmacist, board certified pharmacotherapy specialist, and certified functional medicine practitioner. Dr. Angela is the founder of Cultivate Health & Wellness, a functional medicine practice, with a focus on the gut-brain connection.

Cultivate Health & Wellness serves parents of children and teens, working to identify and reverse the underlying causes of their child's mental health symptoms, including ADHD and anxiety. Dr. Angela uses an integrative approach that includes the gut microbiome, pharmacogenomics, nutrigenomics, and functional lab testing to optimize mental wellness.

Dr. Angela volunteers at the local free health clinic and serves as an adjunct faculty member at Indiana Wesleyan University. Dr. Angela lives on a farm with her husband and two children and enjoys spending time with family, traveling, and cheering on her children. Dr. Angela loves reading and considers herself a life-long learner.

Connect on LinkedIn: www.linkedin.com/in/angela-cates

Schedule a free discovery call: https://calendly.com/angelacates/10min

Trials + Testimony into the Entrepreneurial Journey

My pharmacy career includes work as a clinical pharmacist in a hospital and an ambulatory care clinic before starting my entrepreneurial journey. I loved the one-on-one appointments I had with my patients, and I learned so much from the stories they shared with me during our time together. As time went on, I began to realize that managing medications could only get patients so far on their health journey.

Also, my son began to really struggle with his mental health. His anxiety become so severe that he was refusing to go to school and even ran away from school at one point. I knew I wanted to focus on helping him overcome this and would need a flexible work schedule. I applied for a new position at my facility as a medication safety pharmacist, which included a more flexible schedule and the potential for remote work, but unfortunately, I was not selected for the position. I was disappointed because I had invested a significant amount of time on training to position myself as an expert for the role. Of course, now I can see that God had bigger things planned for me and was closing that door to allow others to open.

I finally found the courage to leave my comfort zone, my job that I knew well with a steady paycheck, benefits, and health insurance for my family. I took a part-time position as a long-term care consultant pharmacist, which allowed me flexibility and to work from home several days per week. It also provided time to create Cates Pharmacy Consulting, LLC, my first business venture, which specialized in medication safety and polypharmacy. I eventually created

Cultivate Health & Wellness, a functional medicine practice with a focus on gut health and mental health through the gut-brain axis.

Share Your Brilliance

My soul gift is nurturing. My patients in the pharmacy often asked if I was a therapist because I was good at sitting and listening to their story. I find myself drawn to people and situations where I can help problem solve and find a path to healing.

My program is based on functional lab testing which is used to identify root causes of disease. The gut is the foundation of our health, so I often start with assessing the gut microbiome and use my RESET Your Gut Health program to help clients. The RESET program includes removing inflammatory triggers such as stress, toxins, and inflammatory foods, eating whole and healing foods, supplementing with gut healing herbs and nutrients, sleep, and exercise to help clients transform their health and their life.

I also use functional lab tests to check micronutrient status and neurotransmitter levels and include nutrigenomic testing to identify genetic vulnerabilities. Based on the lab results and patient symptoms, I work with my clients to create a personalized treatment plan. The plan typically includes targeted nutrition, stress management, physical activity, sleep hygiene, and supplements. I also have a nutritionist as part of my team, and she works with clients to create weekly meal plans and shopping lists to enable them to create sustainable changes.

Overcoming Challenges to Scale

Once I decided to expand my business to include functional medicine, I was not sure where to start, so I joined a six-month intensive pharmacy entrepreneur mentorship program. This program helped me narrow my focus to gut health and enabled me to create the systems and processes that are necessary for a sustainable business. Additionally, I established relationships with other pharmacist entrepreneurs that are still essential to my success today.

After I had the framework in place for my business, then the challenging work really began. Multiple internal blocks came up for me, making it difficult for me to share about my business and attract clients. I dealt with imposter syndrome and unworthiness. I had thoughts like, "Who am I to help people when I am still figuring out my own health and my son's mental health?" Despite completing a functional medicine certification program, I continued to feel that I was not qualified or good enough to help others.

I also struggled to put myself out there and talk about what I could offer. I grew up believing that you should be humble and not brag about yourself, which prevented me from sharing with others how I could help. I did not want to make other people feel uncomfortable by talking about my gifts.

Working through these internal blocks has been a learning process and something I continue to work on. Establishing a daily routine that includes meditation, positive affirmations, and journaling has helped to shift these beliefs and self-doubt. Meeting weekly with a mindset coach has been one of the principal factors in helping me shift my thinking and share what I have to offer with the world. Peeling off the layers to uncover my purpose and how I can serve others has been hard work but extremely rewarding.

Monetizing Your Healing Gifts

During my son's challenges with mental health over the years, I kept thinking that I wanted to do something to help other parents in a similar situation. This led me to expand my functional medication practice to include a focus on mental health with a goal of supporting other parents in finding the root cause and treatments for their child's mental health symptoms.

I work with clients mostly through one-on-one programs. I have created several packages that bundle functional lab testing with consultation and follow-up sessions to provide long-term support resulting in sustainable change.

I have also partnered with an athletic trainer to provide nutrigenomic testing and nutrition counseling for his clients, and I am creating a course that will teach the foundations of gut health to new and potential clients.

What Lights You Up About Your Business

I love being able to help my clients realize they are not alone in the trials that they face. Caring for a child with mental health concerns can feel helpless and isolating. At the peak of my son's anxiety, when he was refusing to go to school, my husband and I felt very isolated from friends and family because no one understood what we were going through. Eventually I was able to connect with another mom who had a similar situation with her son years before. A long conversation with her provided reassurance we were not alone with our challenges and that a positive outcome is possible.

And of course, I also love to help my clients find relief from their mental health and GI symptoms and improve their overall health. When you feel your best, you can be the best version of yourself and share your gifts with the world.

Advice Along the Journey

Find a support system of like-minded entrepreneurs to connect with and learn from. Make time to care for yourself, especially your mental health. Starting a new business will stretch your comfort zone, and enduring the rollercoaster of successes and failures can take a toll if you are not being intentional about separating your value as a person from the results of your business.

What it Means to Be a Heart-Centered Healer in Health Care

To me, being a heart-centered practitioner in healthcare means connecting with my clients on a personal level and empowering them with tools and the information they need to heal on their terms. It also means sharing my own healing journey and the challenges I have overcome to show healing is possible.

Dr. Lisa Zielbauer, fondly known as "Dr. Z," graduated from Midwestern University in 2013 with her doctorate of pharmacy. Shortly after graduation however, she suffered her worst depressive episode and was hospitalized for suicidal ideation.

A few years later, she was fortunate enough to find her passion working as a certified peer counselor at her local NAMI (National Alliance on Mental Illness), where she helped others with mental illness work on their recovery goals.

Yearning to use her degree in an unconventional way, she discovered a new path.

In 2020 she opened her virtual practice, Root Cause Rx, as a Functional Medicine Consultant & Holistic Health Coach after starting her certification through the School of Applied Functional Medicine earlier that year.

Dr. Z helps people with depression relieve their symptoms naturally by maximizing the body's potential to heal itself. Please connect with her on Instagram @RootCauseRx, and to view her services, go here: https://linktr.ee./RootCauseRx

Trials + Testimony into the Entrepreneurial Journey

I was diagnosed with depression and anxiety when I was 18 years old and thought that, if I took my medications and saw my psychiatrist and therapist, things would get better. Unfortunately, I just became depressed again in a couple years. The multiple episodes of depression and medication changes that followed robbed me of years of my life and forced me to take time off from school, quit jobs, and move back home.

A couple of months after graduating from pharmacy school, I went into a deep depression that required hospitalization due to suicidal thoughts. One month later, my dad, who I lived with at the time, unexpectedly passed away from a warfarin (blood thinner) complication after slipping on the ice and hitting his head. This led me down an ever darker, deeper spiral.

After having this lived experience with repetitive cycles of depression relapses for 15+ years, I thought there HAD to be a better way!

After yearning to use my degree, but in an unconventional way, I happened to discover functional medicine (FxMed) in 2019. Treating each person as the unique individual that they are and asking WHY they have these symptoms in the first place just made sense to me. In 2020, I enrolled at the School of Applied Functional Medicine, and later that year, I opened my virtual practice, Root Cause Rx.

Besides applying the FxMed principles to myself, I credit my strong support network and my faith, along with taking time for self-care, including daily nature walks with my dog Lexi, for my successful recovery.

Share Your Brilliance

My innate ability to make others feel at ease, always having an empathic ear to listen, and being sensitive to my word choices so as to not trigger others allows me to form deep connections with others. I am able to listen to another human without judgment, which is something my clients appreciate. My mental illness used to be a deep source of shame for me, but my ability to openly talk about it has become my strength. Vulnerability breeds vulnerability.

I'm all about successful healthy habit building, which I think is the foundation of health, and it all starts with baby steps repeatedly, regularly over time. I work with my clients to find out what they can handle so we don't overwhelm them. That's extremely important, especially for someone with mental health concerns.

The tools I use when working with clients are all based in functional medicine (FxMed) principles. If you're not familiar with FxMed, most other practitioners describe it as holistic medicine, but it is so much more than that. I examine your health down to the cellular level, evaluating the functioning of your entire body from the roots up.

Overcoming Challenges to Scale

Two of my biggest internal challenges while establishing my practice were perfectionism and   imposter syndrome, which tend to go hand in hand.

I would ask myself, "Who am I to help others with depression when I am still on two antidepressants?" I felt like a fraud and thought no one would want to work with me.

Perfectionism kept me from posting more on social media—as I recall one Instagram post in particular took almost 6 hours as I kept correcting the spacing, font, etc. (the downfall of being extremely detail-oriented).

Both of those issues are based on fear. I had fear of the unknown, fear of being seen and judged, fear of failure, AND fear of success. The latter arose because, as many know, with mental illness, one has many episodes over the course of their life. I was afraid of gaining momentum and then not being able to stick with my commitments due to another depressive episode. This led me to dipping my toe in every now and then, but not being willing to give it my all.

How did I overcome all of these automatic negative thoughts (ANTS)?

I made a conscious decision to step INTO my fears instead of around them. My first change was when I moved out from living with my mom. One of my biggest fears since being diagnosed with depression was loneliness. I knew the pain I felt in the past from losing a best friend in junior high, and I didn't want to risk feeling that way again.

I prepared myself by binge-listening to The Imposter Syndrome Terminator podcast by Ines Padar. Even though I was terrified, I kept listening, and I honestly felt a little better and more confident every day. I hadn't seen my therapist for a while surrounding my move, and when I saw her afterwards, she admitted, "I thought you'd be a wreck, but you're fine!" I was fine ... I was better than fine ... in fact, I was great! I had worked through one of my biggest fears and came out triumphant. As I write this, my next therapist appointment is next week and she thinks I've done so well that I don't need to keep seeing her. At first, I felt a pit in my stomach, "But isn't this what someone with mental illness is supposed to do?" I asked. She explained the ultimate goal of any therapist is to see their client use the necessary tools to succeed on their own. "That's the same as functional medicine practitioners!" I exclaimed.

The more action steps I took toward working on my business, the more confident I grew, and the momentum just kept going!

Monetizing Your Healing Gifts

The core of my offerings is 1:1 client consults and coaching three-, six-, and nine-month packages with two meetings a month. I offer other services such as a Nutrigenomics Consult and recently added Mental Health Peer Support, which is non-clinical and similar to my role when I previously worked at NAMI.

An idea that was solidified during Christina's retreat in Florida earlier this year was to start offering 1:1 consults to other heart-centered practitioners who want to start their own flourishing functional medicine (FxMed) practices. I have started doing so and plan to formally open Root Cause Rx Institute sometime next year. This is not a certification like some others offer but is focused solely on the business aspect and starting an FxMed practice.

What Lights You Up About Your Business

Seeing my clients delighted with their results lights me up. I remember one of my first clients messaging me that it was the first time she could recall that she ate three meals in a day, and we celebrated the heck out of her win.

Another client was suffering from low mood and energy with low testosterone. After discovering that his cholesterol levels were also sub-optimally low (yes, I said LOW), we added two eggs to his breakfast (cholesterol is the building block of all sex hormones). After several months, his free testosterone doubled (within the reference range), his low mood lifted, and his energy, including libido, was back! Yeah baby!

Advice Along the Journey

My biggest piece of advice for someone wanting to move beyond traditional medicine into entrepreneurship would be to just start. If I didn't let perfectionism and imposter syndrome delay me from starting my practice, think of all the people I could've helped. As long as you are two steps ahead of someone (which you are), you can help them. You don't need ALL the answers to help someone establish new healthy habits!

What it Means to Be a Heart-Centered Healer in Health Care

Being a heart-centered entrepreneur means always leading with kindness and empathy. It also means taking the time to listen, as well as having integrity and transparency in your offerings.

Financial Coaching

Dr. Anh Evardo, PharmD, BCPS is the founder and CEO of Double Check Bookkeeping LLC, a virtual bookkeeping firm that provides bookkeeping and CFO services to pharmacy entrepreneurs and other small business owners to help them gain financial clarity to scale their businesses. She is passionate about empowering fellow pharmacists in their entrepreneurial journeys.

Dr. Anh is also a clinical pharmacist who currently works in an ambulatory clinic, collaborating with providers to manage chronic disease states, mostly in the endocrinology space. She focuses on helping her patients live healthier lives.

In her free time, Dr. Anh loves spending time with her husband, two kids, and lovable English bulldog; hiking; traveling; and just being outdoors.

You can learn more about Dr. Anh and her bookkeeping and CFO services at https://doublecheckbooks.com.

Trials + Testimony into the Entrepreneurial Journey

A few years ago, my husband started an IT consulting company and was faced with many challenges as a new business owner. One of those challenges was the financial aspect, including the bookkeeping and tax filing. My husband was referred to a "big box" bookkeeping and CPA firm to take care of this piece. At first, my husband was relieved to have an expert handle the bookkeeping and taxes. However, as time went on, he realized the issue with a big box firm—the impersonal attention, the high monthly fees, and the high rate of turnover within the company. There was nobody who asked my husband what his income goals were for the month, quarter, or the year. Nobody to turn to and ask about what the financial reports actually mean and what action plan to take.

There is no worse feeling for a new business owner than to feel lost, defeated, and overwhelmed. Seeing my husband like this, I knew I had to take action. In our family, I already handle the majority of the finances with budgeting, bill pay, and investing. I took bookkeeping courses at the local community college and took over the bookkeeping for my husband's business. That's when we saw my husband's IT consulting company thrive.

I knew that pharmacy entrepreneurs would be in the same shoes that my husband was in just a few years ago. And I knew I could bring the same financial clarity to them. Given my background as a pharmacist, I wanted to help so they could focus on what they do best: helping people feel better. That's when I knew I had to start my bookkeeping firm and focus on fellow pharmacists.

Share Your Brilliance

When it comes to owning a pharmacy business, most pharmacists are not exactly passionate about the ins and outs of bookkeeping and finances. Understandably, pharmacy entrepreneurs are more passionate about their patients and empowering them to live their best lives.

However, understanding the finances of a small business is vital to its success and scalability in the future. As a pharmacist myself, I have the ability to understand the struggles a pharmacy entrepreneur is going through and explain the finances in a way that a pharmacist can understand. Rather than being scared of looking at their numbers, my clients take ownership and dig deep into what the numbers are telling them: where they are spending too much money, where they are making the most profit, what services they should add in the future, etc.

In this way, I help my clients transform and completely shift their mindset when it comes to being the CEO of their business.

Overcoming Challenges to Scale

Growing my bookkeeping firm did not come without challenges. First and foremost, I had major imposter syndrome. I'm a residency-trained clinical pharmacist, not a bookkeeper with an accounting degree! This feeling of not being good enough to handle the bookkeeping for a small business held me back from being successful from the start. I had a fear of failure and of letting down my pharmacy colleagues.

A breakthrough occurred when I finally took my own advice and invested in myself. I invested in a business coach who was a pharmacist herself and coached pharmacists to realize their entrepreneurial dreams. My business coach assured me that my bookkeeping services were indeed needed in the pharmacy field. And in fact, she became my first client in the pharmacy niche.

Empowered with the knowledge that I could make a difference for many pharmacy entrepreneurs and their businesses; I gained the confidence to propel my business forward.

Monetizing Your Healing Gifts

At Double Check Bookkeeping, I offer my clients monthly or quarterly bookkeeping and CFO services. With these done-for-you services, I do all of the bookkeeping, reconciliation of bank accounts, bill pay, payroll, and budgeting. Once a month or quarter, I meet with my clients to review goals, financial reports, and cash flow forecasts.

For the newer entrepreneur who is not quite ready to outsource their bookkeeping, I offer The Balanced Books Bundle, which is bookkeeping done-with-you. With this service, my clients get a two-hour VIP session with me to ensure their books are set up correctly from the start. After this session, clients gain lifetime access to a private Facebook group available only to other pharmacy entrepreneurs who are in the same shoes. This Facebook group has recorded tutorials on bookkeeping basics, direct access to me for questions and support, and monthly office hours via Facebook Live.

Finally, all of my clients gain an accountability partner—me! My clients have a professional bookkeeper in their corner who understands the ins and outs of their pharmacy business.

What Lights You Up About Your Business

Since starting my bookkeeping firm, my absolute favorite part of my business is seeing the powerful mental shift in my clients once they stop fearing their numbers and actually start understanding them, taking ownership of their financials, and being financially responsible so they can scale their businesses beyond their wildest dreams!

Knowing that I made a difference in the mindset of a CEO is so rewarding and drives me to help as many as possible!

Advice Along the Journey

For a business owner just starting on their entrepreneurial journey, be confident in what you can provide for your clients. You have a unique perspective that no other pharmacy entrepreneur has, and this is how you will connect with and heal your clients.

Finally, don't compare your entrepreneurial journey with that of another business owner. As an entrepreneur, your journey will be as different and unique as you are.

What it Means to Be a Heart-Centered Healer in Health Care

Being a heart-centered practitioner in health care means to ensure that each patient or client is also being heart-centered. Our clients should be connecting to themselves and honoring their higher selves in everything they do. We should encourage our clients to listen to their intuition and make choices that are aligned with their values and desires. Only then can we all be confident in our abilities and choices and live a more heart-centered and authentic life.

Health + Lifestyle Coaching

Dr. Melissa Hetrick, PharmD, BCPS, is a clinical staff pharmacist at Lehigh Valley Health Network and a sales coordinator at The Juice Plus + Company. She currently specializes in hematology/oncology at the LVHN Topper Cancer Institute. She practiced within the inpatient setting for the first 15 years of her career, focusing on areas such as pediatrics, parenteral nutrition, operating room satellite, and intravenous compounding.

Dr. Melissa guides hard-working women down a clear path of health and wellness, replacing unfavorable habits with simple changes to attain confidence and balance. Her dream is to help these women and their families learn how to prevent disease with food as their medicine, rather than treating it with an overload of prescription medications.

For more information on joining Dr. Melissa's mission and finding healing for yourself, email Melissa_HealthyHabits@outlook.com.

Trials + Testimony into the Entrepreneurial Journey

In 2015, I started to become disenchanted with the world of healthcare. I had begun the long and arduous journey of intravenous fertilization (IVF) treatments, which lasted three years, three cycles, and no baby to hold at the end. The process made me feel lost, unsupported, unimportant, and alone. I had minimal support, and counseling was merely a suggestion. The despair and desperation are something I never want another woman to endure.

In the fertility office, not a single woman acknowledged the woman next to them, even though we were all there for the same reason. It was one of the strangest experiences I've had. The healthcare system made it feel impersonal and difficult to express and share our individual needs; It was quite a lonely place to be! Even as a pharmacist, I didn't understand the financial aspect and quickly ran out of funds. As a result, my husband and I incurred thousands of dollars in medical bills and denied claims.

My personal disheartening experience with the healthcare system shed light on what I really wanted for my professional future, and I felt as though I was destined for more. My relationship with Juice Plus + began while I was looking to become healthier during IVF; it was just one of the many different modalities I tried, along with gluten- and dairy-free diets, acupuncture, root vegetable juices, Chinese herbs, supplements, and yoga. When I started to focus on whole food nutrition through Juice Plus +, I realized I could help my friends and family prevent disease versus treating it. My goal is to help women realize that it's okay to prioritize and take time for themselves, and The Juice Plus+ Company has given me the direction and mission to do so, as well as continue to foster my love of helping people as a pharmacist.

Share Your Brilliance

As women, we rarely put ourselves first because we question our self-worth and don't believe we are our own number one priority. By using my positive spirit, heart-centered attitude, and a healthy dose of laughter, I'm able to lead women down a clear path of health and wellness, replacing unfavorable habits with simple changes to attain confidence and balance. I believe in hearing every woman's story and placing myself in their shoes, so I can find the right plan for them. The transformation begins with whole food nutrition focused on increased intake of plant-based foods and small daily changes. The foundation of my work with women includes deep breathing, practicing self-love through dedicated mindfulness techniques, food prepping, and participating in a community of like-minded people.

Overcoming Challenges to Scale

My initial introduction to exploring the meaning behind the commonly heard phrase, "I don't have enough time," was working with Rebekah "Bex" Borucki, founder of BexLife. Through her four-minute meditations, mentoring program, and down-to-earth personality, I began to see how time management was something I needed to improve upon. I realized that it wasn't about not having the time to reach my goals, but rather choosing what to do with the time I had available. This was a major "aha" moment for me. Saying that we don't have time for something often means that we really don't want to do it right then, and guess what … *that's okay.* I have been challenged with figuring out when to focus on my business, my family, volunteer work, self-care, and mindfulness practices; however, I have learned to acknowledge my desires for the time I have by creating boundaries, devoting blocks of time for my business, and communicating with my family.

Monetizing Your Healing Gifts

As a Juice Plus+ direct sales consultant, I can use my passion for helping women by having individual conversations, listening to their pain points, and curating a package of supplements tailored to their needs. My program includes regular checkups for not only adherence, but also to make sure my clients are having a positive experience at 10, 30, 90, and 120 days.

Free educational content, developed by my team, includes webinars, in-person events, Facebook Live videos, and a YouTube channel called "Healthy Habits with the Sisters," which is a collaboration between my sister, Jennifer Judd, and me. I adore answering questions from my clients because questions help us grow and expand our minds so we can become our own healthcare advocates. Through the Juice Plus+ Company, I can offer individualized and group coaching with a program called *Shred10*, which focuses on 10 simple guidelines spanning 10 days. Clients can join our community Facebook page to receive the support of hundreds of consultants from all walks of life. Everyone is invited into the community and is given the option to join our team for additional rebates and rewards.

What Lights You Up About Your Business

The clients that light me up are the women with slow transformations, who the concepts don't immediately "click" for. We all struggle day after day to break unwelcome habits, either ingrained from childhood or developed in today's fast-paced world. Picture a mom with kids who are picky eaters and a busy spouse. Getting food on the table and constantly juggling day-to-day activities is a considerable stressor. This hard-working woman doesn't put herself first and can't picture herself as a priority. Sticking with my program and making simple daily changes has the potential to unlock a side of her that she didn't know longed to be released. When she realizes that finding a balance between a busy life and her own health and wellness is essential, it's pure gold. The lightbulb of understanding comes on and ... *BOOM* ... she becomes ablaze with self-actualization, and I just love it!

Advice Along the Journey

Exploring resources beyond traditional medicine can be scary, confusing, and overwhelming, but that doesn't mean it isn't time for a change. I would advise any woman, especially those considering entrepreneurship, to find a daily mindfulness practice. Slowing down and opening the mind provides the opportunity to remove distractions, allowing the Universe to present its plan. I prefer a mix of yoga, meditation, simple deep breathing, and hypnosis. It may be challenging with our busy lives and overactive minds, but strive to find a quiet getaway from the noise, infuse a pleasing scent into your routine, and gift yourself a daily practice. Sometimes, inner work is needed most to reveal what is holding you back and dimming your light. Striking out on your own with a new business takes time, patience, and diligence to create the magic that is your unique path, but know that you are worth it, you can do it *your* way, and don't be afraid to take a chance! You are no longer alone on this important journey.

What it Means to Be a Heart-Centered Healer in Health Care

Dr. Christina Fontana has guided me to discover and release the internal blocks I was carrying, like perfectionism, guilt, feeling unworthy, and being afraid to shine. Using her unique method, my gifts have blossomed, allowing me to practice my business using a heart-centered approach. I can coach women based on my core values and beliefs, offering layers of expertise, along with growing and learning with them. My vision of a heart-centered practitioner is someone who listens completely, who is living her passion, and who wants her clients to heal with ease. Time is not a limitation in her practice, and she supports her clients nutritionally, medically, and holistically.

Johnnie Kemp, R.Ph. is the CEO of Pharmedix, LLC. She is also the creator of The Biohack Your Body METHOD™ where she helps clients achieve optimal health and even reverse their biological age through a personalized approach to epigenetic modification.

Johnnie is also part of an elite global team of certified NeuroChangeSolutions Consultants for Dr. Joe Dispenza, to teach powerful and sustainable transformation to individuals, businesses and organizations.

Johnnie has over 25+ years of diverse experience in healthcare, including pharmaceutical sales, clinical consulting, and home infusion and was the owner of Space Coast Assisted Living, LLC.

By leveraging her healthcare experience with a holistic approach based on neuroscience, she has curated a program to help her clients achieve true transformation in body, mind, and spirit.

To learn more, please visit Johnnie's website at www.goholistichealth.com.

You can also reach her at https://www.linkedin.com/in/johnnierph

Trials + Testimony into the Entrepreneurial Journey

Before I was able to become a heart-centered health care practitioner who could help others, I had to look at my own heart wounds, acknowledge them, hug and love that little girl who was still hurting, and help her understand she doesn't have to be afraid anymore. I know she has been trying to keep me safe so we won't get hurt. And I love her for trying to protect us. We both had to go through struggles and learn lessons. People hurt us, even tried to destroy us, but we survived. We may have gotten knocked down and bruised. We may have bent, but we did not break.

We survived. I survived.

For many years, I asked myself, "Do you want to be a victim, or do you want to be a survivor? Choose one." "I am a survivor"—that was my personal theme song; Beyoncé sang that just for me.

As a single mom raising three daughters, I knew I needed to be strong.

I didn't always know how, but I could pretend. I could pretend to be strong, so my daughters wouldn't see the worries and fear, so they wouldn't feel the heartache that almost crushed me. After all, this was not an easy time for them either. So, one day at a time, I pretended to be strong. And sometimes it was true.

After all, I had done this before.

My childhood was bitter-sweet. I grew up as an only child in a blue collar family in Mississippi. I was lucky. My parents loved me, especially my very protective mom. I knew she loved me; after all, I was her "chosen child." I was adopted as a baby. I still remember a verse from a poem my mom used to read, "You didn't grow under my heart, but in it."

I knew I was loved, but why did I feel so unlovable? What did I do wrong? Why did my birth mother just give me away? Why didn't she want me? Why didn't she love me? Maybe she was just a teenager who ran away from home and didn't know how to take care of a baby; maybe she was really a Native American princess that had been kidnapped.

Those thoughts, that fear of abandonment and rejection, fear of unworthiness gradually became beliefs. Most times, I could push the thoughts away, and as a young child, I had fun memories of playing with cousins and friends, and parents who kissed me and tucked me in bed at night.

Then came the teen years, and because I excelled in academics, my parents scrimped to pay for a private school where I received a great education. However, many classmates were quite unkind to this young girl who must have worn her insecurity like a large scarlet letter. I didn't really fit in with the children of the wealthier families, who wore the right clothes, and said witty things, and I certainly wasn't welcome in their cliques. There was a lot of teasing and buckets of tears, but I found a refuge in science. I poured myself into what evolved into a multi-year science project that ultimately led to a college scholarship. Interestingly enough, this project involved an in-depth study of adrenal gland hormones and their effects on the body. This is something I would later reflect on as one of life's synchronicities and a preparation for what would lie ahead.

Fast forward to pharmacy school where I found acceptance and even became president of Kappa Epsilon. I had a successful and diverse career in pharma sales, clinical consulting, managing home infusion pharmacies, and owning two small assisted living facilities.

I married and was the primary breadwinner, had three wonderful daughters, divorced, supported my daughters, and put them all through college. After all, I am a survivor. Failure is not an option.

So, I decided to give marriage a second try, and now looking back with a clearer perspective, I can see that my decision was influenced by what had become part of my belief system, my programming, that I was not really worthy of true love. After only two years of marriage, I received the shock of my life as the facades and tower of deceit came tumbling down. I immediately filed for divorce and, amid death threats, FBI watch lists, and drama that could make an entire

Netflix series, I fled. I moved across the state, found a new job, and started rebuilding my life.

Being a survivor just took on a whole new meaning.

Share Your Brilliance

As it turned out, moving was the best thing that happened FOR me. New doors opened, and walking through them changed the trajectory of my life.

I attended a biohacking conference and fell in love with epigenetics and optimizing health. I embraced a holistic approach to our bodies as a wonderful interconnected system, and it appealed to my "less is more" and "risk vs benefit" philosophy when it comes to prescription medications. I was inspired to start a health coaching business so I could help others. This has evolved into my group coaching program that I created called "The Biohack Your METHOD™" where I teach women how to actually reverse biological age, and uplevel their health.

The second door that opened was discovering Dr. Joe Dispenza. One word: life-changing. I resonate with how the neurochemistry of our thoughts signals the hormones of stress in the adrenal glands, and the hormones affect our gene expression, and of course, gene expression affects every cell in our bodies. I was instantly hooked. It appealed to my geeky scientific brain. There was much more to come.

Overcoming Challenges to Scale

I had to learn to quiet my brain, to recognize those stories I had been telling *myself* the stories that put up walls to protect me from being rejected, the stories that told me I was unwanted and unworthy. That was hard! That was uncomfortable! But if I could silence those voices and go into the river of change, I could connect with the divine energy of the Universe, energy that is also inside me, then I can step into my new life as my new empowered self. And so I have!

Monetizing Your Healing Gifts

Dr. Joe has a company called NeuroChangeSolutions. Frankly, I didn't know very much about it, but I knew I wanted to be part of it. So, I put my intention out into the Universe, and I imagined what it would feel like to be an NCS consultant. I felt happiness and gratitude in my heart ahead of the event, even though I had no idea if my application would be accepted. The Universe said "YES!" I recently returned from Cancun where I completed training as an NCS consultant.

What Lights You Up About Your Business

By the time this book is published, I will be fully licensed to teach Dr. Joe Dispena's workshops to businesses and organizations to help "Change Your Mind ... Create New Results." Sharing the work that has changed my life and knowing that I have found my purpose and can inspire and help others is a dream come true.

Advice Along the Journey

I went from victim to survivor. It served me well.

The next evolution was from survivor to creator. That's where the magic happens, where infinite possibilities exist. You can do it too!

What it Means to Be a Heart-Centered Healer in Health Care

To live and to share Love, Light, and Healing—

You are greater than you think,

More powerful than you know,

More unlimited than you could ever dream.

Dr. Joe Dispenza

Dr. Sarah Meyers is the founder of Lifestyle Rx, LLC—an all-encompassing health and wellness coaching program. She helps women prioritize their health and self-care needs so they can create a lifestyle full of confidence, energy, and joy! She is a NSCA certified personal trainer and a Precision Nutrition certified nutrition coach. Dr. Sarah earned her doctor of pharmacy degree from the University of Buffalo School of Pharmacy and Pharmaceutical Sciences. She has over 17 years of experience in the retail pharmacy setting.

Sarah enjoys lifting weights, running, and being creative in the kitchen. She currently lives in western New York with her husband and two children. However, she often finds herself dreaming of sunshine and palm trees.

To reach Sarah, please visit her Instagram profile @ssm7707

If interested in working with Lifestyle Rx, LLC, visit http://lifestylerxwithsarah.com for a free consult.

Trials + Testimony into the Entrepreneurial Journey

A long time ago, someone told me to "stop trying to be something, because you're not." My anger was turned inward. My diet became disordered and obsessive—a coping mechanism that came about oh, so innocently. It was the start of the self-harm and self-hate. I experienced years of abuse and betrayal—and I internalized it all to be my fault. I hid my pain behind perfectionism, achievements, and a "cheerleader smile." Behind closed doors was also the private shame that came with an eating disorder, and as I discovered wine, from alcohol abuse.

Fast forward many years, and my eyes were opened to a new way of living, which completely changed my life. By joining an online fitness challenge, my dysfunctional eating and drinking habits slowly faded away. I focused my attention on fueling my body with balanced nutrition and moving my body consistently. I gained energy, confidence, and self-respect and simply felt "dancing-in-the-kitchen-good" by prioritizing myself and treating myself better, one day at a time.

My transformation became the catalyst that led me where I am today—reframing healthcare to include more acts of self-care.

As my physical health had greatly improved, I began implementing various tools to balance out other areas of wellness. I focused on my *mental* and *emotional wellbeing* by starting therapy, meditation practice, and journaling and allowing myself to express emotions that had been long suppressed. I worked on balancing *social wellness* by attending dinners out with friends and enjoying travel. I fostered *intellectual wellness* by enrolling in certification programs in personal training and nutrition. I worked on my *spiritual wellness* by leaning into the bigger picture and trusting that I was supported. And lastly, after feeling the tug on my heartstrings and spending many days feeling misaligned in the retail pharmacy setting, I decided to advance my *occupational wellbeing* by leaping forward into entrepreneurship!

Using the foundation of my own transformation, I created Lifestyle Rx, an all-encompassing health and wellness coaching program designed to meet clients where they are with their unique needs, strengths, and struggles. We work on various daily self-care practices in all areas of wellness—blending mind, body, and soul. I help women find that spark that at times seems so dim. I support them in creating a lifestyle that feels balanced and nourished.

Share Your Brilliance

I see women struggle with their weight and eating behaviors, constantly trying every new diet, only to yo-yo back and forth.

I see women living sedentary lives as they've exhausted all of their energy being caretakers to others.

I see women wanting to be "toned" but not knowing how to start with strength training.

I see women escaping into a socially acceptable bottle of wine, only to wake the next day feeling groggy and with regret.

I see women buying the pretty journals, only to stare at blank pages ... after all, if they can't do it (or anything) perfectly, why bother.

I see women going to their healthcare providers to quickly have their concerns dismissed and going home without being heard.

I *see* these women because I was once one of them. I know the pain that these feelings bring when all you want to do is wake feeling energized, feel good in your skin, and know that your best (regardless of what it looks like on that day) is enough! You want to live a healthy lifestyle that allows you to live life to its fullest ... and occasionally eat a donut without any guilt!

I tune in to these women and see the deeper transformation possibilities. I listen empathetically. I lead by example showing the value in consistency, perseverance, and resiliency.

We start with small daily practices of self-care, which cultivates confidence.

We respect our bodies with food and beverages that are nutritious, delicious, yet moderate.

We invite in movement that we enjoy.

We set goals.

We set boundaries.

We celebrate ourselves—Yay Me!

We create sacred time to listen to our inner voice.

We practice mindfulness and gratitude.

We move away from the all-or-nothing/good-bad mentality and lean in toward neutrality.

We discover grace in the gray.

We reframe challenges and perceived failures as areas of opportunities.

We show up for ourselves every. f*cking. day.

Overcoming Challenges to Scale

My biggest challenge was feeling as though I have not yet healed myself enough to help others.

I've worked on embodying my self-worth. I've released the resistance to expressing vulnerability and allowing the truest version of myself to be seen. I share the message of my mess, let my pain be of purpose, and use the wisdom of my wounds to be a radiant light to those still in the dark.

As part of the deep inner work, I became comfortable standing on my own. I had always worked for a corporation and am affiliated with a well-established fitness community. I cultivated self-trust and listened to my intuition—to know that my voice, truth, beliefs and values were worthy to promote on their own. I spent time in meditation focusing on self-trust and alignment. I was introduced to other female pharmacist entrepreneurs through Dr. Christina Fontana and the Elevate Entrepreneur Academy. We were all doing the same thing— following our hearts and venturing out on our own. The support here and from the fitness community has been reassuring when self-doubt tries to creep in. I am forever grateful for these connections, as they have allowed me to embrace and advocate for changes that improve patient care, yet are beyond that of the traditional pharmacist role.

Monetizing Your Healing Gifts

Lifestyle Rx, LLC, offers two tiers of 1:1 high-level accountability coaching. The client has the option to choose between a nutritional and lifestyle coaching program or a package that adds on personalized strength training. These options are designed to create long-term, sustainable changes through self-care practices, habit formation, and mindset shifts. Clients receive daily messaging, guidance, encouragement, feedback, redirection, and virtual check-ins.

What Lights You Up About Your Business

It brings me great joy to see clients celebrate themselves, take pride in their choices, and reclaim ownership over their lives. I love watching the daily practices transform into habits. Those habits are then built upon, creating expansive results over time. I love seeing them achieve and transform that which they didn't think was possible—proving that they *do* have the power within to change. They've always had it!

I love offering a deeper level of connection via 1:1 engagement. Clients receive the time and attention they deserve (often unavailable in today's healthcare settings) where the intimate details of their lives are seen, heard, and connected. It creates a safe space for the clients to grow and heal at their own pace. I love seeing that lightbulb moment when it comes to fruition that honoring *all* aspects of wellbeing is fundamental in creating a deeper transformation, leading to the lifestyle they desire.

Advice Along the Journey

CHOOSE YOUR HARD:

You can settle for a secure and predictable role, doing what is expected, and not dispensing your full potential.

--OR--

You can venture into the uncertainty, trusting and surrendering, knowing that you are supported when leading from the heart. There are people out there who need your unique gifts.

Take the **L.E.A.P.**— **L**et go. **E**levate. **A**lign with your **P**urpose.

What it Means to Be a Heart-Centered Healer in Health Care

It means turning inward and listening to your desires, for the heart is the keeper of your truth. And when you act from authenticity, you will best be able to serve. Lifestyle Rx was created in alignment with my values and gifts, strengthened by my personal experiences and resiliency, to lead by example, and elevate healthcare through self-care and self-love.

Dr. Beth Thomas, PharmD, RPh is a digital health consultant, a licensed pharmacist, and the CEO of BMT Consulting Services, LLC (previously BMT Coaching). She is also an American Fitness Professionals & Associates (AFPA)-certified weight management specialist and nutrition and wellness consultant.

Her weight struggles inspired her to start her own company, focused on helping busy women harness the power of nutrition for permanent health and weight transformation. In 2020, AFPA named Dr. Beth's company as one of seven black-owned health and fitness businesses that are changing the industry.

After experiencing coaching success, she became passionate about serving organizations with all she has created so they can multiply her results through their platforms. Dr. Beth now uses her expertise to help digital health companies leverage effective, evidence-based content, courses, and collaboration solutions for faster growth and more significant impact. Follow her on Instagram @drbethconsulting.

Trials + Testimony into the Entrepreneurial Journey

I struggled with my weight from childhood to early adulthood. My business was born to share everything I learned during my final weight loss journey and in my work as a pharmacist to help busy women like me permanently transform their weight.

Although exercising made me feel good, I realized that my food choices made the difference on the scale. I also discovered that healthy eating does not have to be time-consuming or complicated. Furthermore, nutrition impacts the way we feel, think, work, and interact with others.

Leveraging everything I've learned about nutrition, I've been maintaining my approximately 25- to 30-pound weight loss for eight years and counting. As a result, my mental, physical, and emotional health have improved enormously. My passion is helping as many women as possible, especially those in the black community, permanently transform their weight, health, and lives through the power of food.

Share Your Brilliance

My firm yet loving coaching style has been the most crucial factor in getting glowing testimonials from my coaching clients and establishing myself as a leader in my field. Additionally, my special three-part healthy meal formula allows women to achieve their weight and health goals without being overwhelmed.

Furthermore, one of my healing gifts is helping women discover the true meaning of consistency as the pathway to permanent transformation. I find that many women are perfectionists. They often feel they must complete a long list of simultaneous changes to achieve weight loss and better health. My unique consistency-based coaching approach has helped numerous women realize that success will come when they focus on doing at least one thing every day, no matter how "small" it may seem, to move forward. This simple but powerful mindset shift is a game changer!

As a digital health consultant, I now apply these practical and proven methods and tools to tailor health management programs for companies so they can multiply my coaching results through their platforms.

Overcoming Challenges to Scale

One of the biggest obstacles I've faced in building my business is being a black woman in a white-dominated space. Systemic racism has meant minimal access to critical funding, a limited business support network, and marketing hardships for me (and other black entrepreneurs).

Slavery, as well as local, state, and federal laws and policies in the decades following the Emancipation Proclamation excluded black people from asset-building opportunities while simultaneously providing innumerable opportunities for white people to accumulate generational wealth-building resources (financial, land, educational, social, etc.).

Consequently, my lack of "acceptable" financial and social capital has closed many doors on my entrepreneurship journey. Handling all the responsibilities of managing my business and dealing with the numerous challenges of being a black business owner can sometimes feel overwhelming. However, I can genuinely say that my faith is the only thing that has kept me going. Relying on God for strength and remembering my "why" have helped me remain consistent and keep pushing forward during times of discouragement.

Monetizing Your Healing Gifts

For over eight years, I helped busy women (specifically those with 30 or more pounds to lose) permanently transform their weight and lives. I did this by teaching them to harness the power of food through my consistency-focused coaching programs. Eventually, I had a vast library of effective, evidence-based videos, worksheets, workshops, and other resources that helped my clients achieve their health goals.

I then realized I could impact even more lives by forming strategic partnerships with other organizations, mainly digital health platforms. These companies aim to improve health outcomes for the people they serve, but they often try to do everything themselves. As a result, they spend precious time creating programming from scratch rather than leveraging proven solutions.

I now use my expertise to provide customized content, course, and collaboration solutions to digital health platforms, giving them a faster path for growth.

What Lights You Up About Your Business

With my current digital consulting practice, I love the hands-on interactions with my clients. Assessing companies' current setups and highlighting their specific growth opportunities for increased income and impact are fulfilling tasks.

As part of my work, I also enjoy tailoring content and courses for digital health platforms. Being a natural-born educator and researcher, tweaking programming solutions to help these companies elevate their brands is fun for me.

Advice Along the Journey

Identify your mission, values, and priorities as an entrepreneur and remain faithful to them. Record them, and keep them someplace visible so you can refer to them often and so you never forget your "why." Doing this will help you on those hard days when you want to quit or consider doing something that may not align with your business vision.

What it Means to Be a Heart-Centered Healer in Healthcare

Being a heart-centered practitioner in healthcare means showing up as my entire, authentic self in everything I do. I'm a black female with unique and valuable life experiences, who is intimately familiar with the adverse effects of systemic racism in the healthcare system.

Also, I have a burning desire to educate women about the power of food for positive mental, emotional and physical health. I unabashedly promote proper nutrition as the first line of defense against disease.

Dr. Melissa Thompson is passionate about possibility. A lifelong learner, she holds a doctorate in pharmacy, a master of arts in counseling psychology, and a certificate in expressive arts. She has studied yoga, meditation, integrative medicine, and creative expression. Dr. Melissa serves the individual on the journey to creating, cultivating, and celebrating a life they love living by blending these modalities of personal growth into the services she offers.

As a spiritual alchemist, Dr. Melissa fuses her years of life learning and experience as a clinical pharmacist with her passion for creative expression to dive deep into the roots of life. Her mission is to help others cultivate the soil of their soul and celebrate the sacred beauty of human potential. Her curious mind has led to the discovery of creative opportunities—seeds of potentiality—cultivated and celebrated in a life that blooms with full vibrancy.

Please contact her through email: melissa@createcultivatecelebrate.com.

Trials + Testimony into the Entrepreneurial Journey

Create Cultivate Celebrate is more than a business; it is a mantra and a way of life. I reached a point in my career when I left everything and drove off in my car on a journey to know myself to the core. I participated in meditation retreats and lived in intentional communities. During this time, I learned about who I was on the inside.

What prompted my journey into the internal unknown? My desire to connect with the creative aspects of myself and to heal my heart. I had an ache, the kind that doesn't go away, that kept telling me that there was more to living this life than accepting the daily grind.

I believe in the power of our innate potential as humans. We have a capacity to grow and expand beyond what we thought possible. My desire is to help others connect with that potential.

Share Your Brilliance

In working with clients, I use my natural strengths to connect with and walk alongside the individual in their personal growth life cycle.

I do this by providing the following:

Empathic listening and responding.

Strategic solutions. I see creative solutions quickly and teach clients how to implement them.

Development of personal goals and the steps to achieve them. I accomplish this by meeting the person where they are in their own personal growth life cycle.

Positivity. The power of innate positivity is often overlooked. This is not about sweeping things under the rug or putting on rose-colored glasses. This is about a paradigm shift and holding a perspective that can bring an enormous amount of energy flow to life.

Individualization. I can see the unique gifts in others and the potential they hold to find solutions that will allow them to create, cultivate, and celebrate a life they love living.

I am a relationship builder, and with my inherent ability to connect and work with others, I find that clients and I can move into material and through challenges quickly. I use metaphors and visualizations that transport the client into their healing element and open the doors for them to identify creative solutions for their life.

Service is at the center of my heart. This is what drew me from the science labs and into the pharmacy. Compassionate care has always been at the center of my work ethic.

Overcoming Challenges to Scale

Growing a business takes grit and stamina. My process has been focused on tending the soil of my soul. To be the gardener of my life and business, the first step was to amend the soil. For the nutrients to make an impact on the earth, the previous soil must be broken down, opened, and turned over before adding new soil to strengthen its vitality. Building my business has taken me to my core, and I have revisited the practices and resources that initiated my journey. The "opening" of the soil has been a practice of letting go of what others think and finding the calling that I wrote about when I was 16 years old.

In a journal from a vision fast I participated in during high school, I wrote:

I hope to become successful, not only in material wealth, but wealth in love, knowledge, and creativity. In whatever profession I choose to advance in, I want to be happy in what I am doing. I want to be challenged and looked up to as an outstanding businesswoman. I want to use my artistic talents. I want to enjoy getting up each day, to be able to realize the gift that I have, life itself.

This theme was repeated in a vision fast in my adult life that I articulate in my book Seeds of Potentiality: A Guide to the Life Cycle of Personal Growth as this:

By bringing my presence and nurturing love to the care of my body, mind, and soul, I am tending to my life, my garden. The garden that I have the ultimate responsibility to tend and cultivate. The devotion and attention that I put into choosing the foods I eat, the words I speak, and the activities I participate in have a foundational influence on the quality of my days and nights. By finding my creative flow, igniting the fire in the clearing, turning the soil, and allowing my roots to push through, I arrived at the sunrise in the garden of my life with an outpouring of love.

The amendment that I have incorporated into the soil of my soul contains acceptance, joy, creativity, and more. Each nutrient enriches my body, mind, and spirit. This becomes the wellspring of nourishment I have to offer others.

Monetizing Your Healing Gifts

The outpouring of my transformation as a coach and business owner is my book Seeds of Potentiality: A Guide to the Life Cycle of Personal Growth. This book integrated the layers of my life and the various healing experiences into a coherent picture. Utilizing imagery from a vision fast, I weave a story that portrays the life cycle of personal growth. From this paradigm, I then offer creative solutions to everyday living. The ideas come from a tapestry of experiences and resources that I describe throughout the book.

To further integrate and offer growth opportunities to others, I offer individual coaching. Online courses are on their way, and my new vision is a nourishing retreat experience.

What Lights You Up About Your Business

Creativity. The soul is inherently creative, and when we connect with our creativity, we see that our ability to be resilient in this life is endless. This is what carries humans through war, famine, pandemics, conflicts, personal struggles, and disappointments. Using the visual, audio, tactile, and other senses opens our ability to connect beyond the thought-based life we are used to living. Dropping into an embodiment of how we want to live and feel offers a deep-felt sense of how we want to live our lives.

My tagline has naturally become, "Live a life you love living." Only the individual can describe this, and when you identify what living a life you love looks like, it becomes an adventure that can be embraced.

When a client's face lights up from the internal connection with their own passion, their own why, I feel this in my heart, and my drive to keep working with individuals in their personal growth journey strengthens.

Advice Along the Journey

Find your "why," and take the steps to live out your passion. Hear the call, and act upon it.

My process has taken years. The fear of allowing myself to embrace what my 16-year-old self knew held me back. I contained my gifts. I hid my light. She has spoken to me and said, "Now is the time."

Work the soil of your soul and allow yourself to integrate all the aspects of your life. The whole person you desire to be in this life will emerge and bloom.

What it Means to Be a Heart-Centered Healer in Health Care

To be a heart-centered healer in health care means living out your truth. If we continue to hide in our fears and hold back our gifts, we hide the healing we have to offer. We may also hide solutions and new avenues for healing. The landscape of how we heal has evolved. Wisdom from various traditions and cultures immigrated into the mainstream and our communities; the individuals we serve are looking for new avenues to heal. Meet them on the path, bring your gifts, and shine your light.

Spiritual Life Coaching

Dr. Nina Castle, PharmD, is a spiritual life coach and holistic pharmacist. She is the founder and CEO of Soul Harmony LLC. She is certified as a life coach, 6-Phase Meditation trainer, integrative pharmacist specialist, and pharmacogenomics pharmacist.

Dr. Nina brings calm to wounded souls. She helps Christians desiring increased spiritual awareness (or who are moving through a spiritual transformation) to navigate so they can develop a closer connection with God. Although her work is designed for Christians, it can benefit anyone.

Her desire is to offer hope and healing by instilling a sense of calm and harmony, removing the veil, and opening the door for increased insight and self-awareness, aiding in healing a soul's wounds and straightening the path to a deeper connection with God.

Each person's story is for God's glory.

To help you with your story of hope and healing: www.DrNinaCastle.com

Trials + Testimony into the Entrepreneurial Journey

I considered becoming an entrepreneur years before I finally did. I strongly dislike giving my time, energy, loyalty, and compassion to employers who do not value employees. I always preferred a holistic approach to healing. Pharmacy was not always fulfilling, and I was restricted in how I could help heal others.

The determining challenge of entrepreneurship was my need to step out of the FEAR of leaving my detrimental pharmacist job and step into a life of freedom, flow, and FAITH. The financial concerns and the "golden handcuffs" kept me chained to a "comfort zone" of discomfort. After the death of a fellow pharmacist, it was eye-opening to realize how replaceable we were. The poor morale, extreme burnout, and health issues caused by work led toward destruction. This was certainly not a way anyone should live. (If you are working somewhere and feel like you are barely surviving, you are putting your soul at dis-ease and dis-comfort, and something needs to change.) I could no longer work there. It was the final push off the diving board of fear, into the unknown—faith. Falling into the depths of the unknown, surprisingly, provided a sense of relief and freedom, even without having a plan intricately mapped out—and this is coming from a control-and-planning freak! I trusted God to provide the next steps. (Come on in—the "water" is fine!)

I ache for the world to have more hope and healing. I long for us all to experience ever-increasing awareness of ourselves—such as from understanding how stress impacts our health and behavior or by learning to love ourselves unconditionally—along with a more intimate connection with God, who adores us. I pray that we thrive and shine—not remain "stuck" in situations or mindsets that fragment our souls. I want vitality and healing for our souls—*soul harmony*. This is my journey, too.

Share Your Brilliance

I bring healing and calm to wounded souls through spoken and written words, the music and lyrics of my songs, singing, a soothing touch, or simply by being physically near someone. This has been an ongoing theme throughout my life; the weaving of examples as vibrant-colored threads form a beautiful tapestry representing my soul-aligned purpose.

My blog provides insight into things I've experienced that may encourage those encountering similar situations. What we've endured in this life can help others—our story is for God's glory.

I bridge together thoughts, concepts, and emotions to create a flow that draws people to a deeper spiritual level and a more intimate relationship with God.

I see and speak truth, using wisdom and discernment, with humility and thankfulness.

As an empath, I've numbed myself from pain and emotions. I know that I must have proper boundaries and "feel to heal," as must my clients.

I solve problems and provide a safe, compassionate, nurturing, comforting, and non-judgmental environment to guide clients toward solutions.

I have deeply-rooted faith from relying on God through life's heartaches.

I am learning to let go of control, fear, and worry; what you focus on expands, and these things serve no purpose!

I am practicing self-love as the beginning of true peace and healing.

I help Christians desiring increased spiritual awareness (or who are moving through a spiritual transformation) to navigate so they can develop a closer connection with God.

Although my work is designed with Christians in mind, all are welcome to experience the hope and healing that I want to offer the world.

Tools I use with clients incorporate prayer and/or Scriptures (optional for 1:1 coaching):

- Meditation
- Prayer
- Emotional Freedom Technique (tapping)
- Visualization (guided meditation)
- Affirmations
- Breathwork
- Polyvagal Theory
- Energy Medicine (general techniques)

Overcoming Challenges to Scale

My internal blocks dissuade me from moving forward as quickly as I would like in my business: perfectionism, fear of criticism/failure/being seen. As I work through these blocks, their hold on me lessens. Their arrows' painful strikes to my soul become duller and fewer over time and easier to pluck from my soul so healing can become permanent. It's an ongoing process, but an upward spiral to healing and soul harmony.

Programs, meditations, prayer, and books increase my self-awareness, engage me in shadow work, keep my soul anchored to God, and help process the painful emotions that were barricaded over the years—feelings that were repressed and suppressed, causing chronic stress. I strive to be a better version of myself and to love myself unconditionally.

The Happy PharmD and Dr. Jamie Wilkey were instrumental at the contemplation stage of my entrepreneurial journey. (Check them out!)

Dr. Christina Fontana's coaching was fundamental as I stood on the diving board of fear and leapt with faith into the unknown. (Even coaches need a coach!)

I became a certified life coach and 6-Phase Meditation trainer through MindValley/EverCoach. (As a coach, you coach yourself first!)

I'm blessed to have communities with pharmacist entrepreneurs and life coaches. There are many mentor-worthy coaches and speakers who helped pave the path of my journey.

I have constant gratitude for the love, support, and refining from my immediate family, my church family, and from Creator God, the Holy Spirit, and my example, Jesus Christ.

Monetizing Your Healing Gifts

I am or will be offering the following to help and bless others:

- Poems/songs for home/office décor and inspiration
- Meditation collections (audio and visual)
- Online courses
- Workshops
- Group coaching
- 1:1 coaching (prayer/Scripture optional)
- Meditation/wellness retreats (future dream!)
- A musical with a message of hope and healing based on a true story (in process!)

What Lights You Up About Your Business

It brings me joy to help others elevate to an improved way of feeling and being.

From instilling a sense of calm and harmony in one's soul, removing the veil and opening the door for increased insight and self-awareness, and aiding in healing a soul's wounds, to straightening the path to a deeper connection with God—I am honored and grateful for God to use me to help others.

Advice Along the Journey

Advice that helped me, so it may help you—

Faith over fear: Take that leap of faith; the fear does not serve you and will keep you shackled, "comfortable" in your discomfort, and will eat away at your soul. That is no way to live! Fear is not going to help you help others. Do NOT let fear hold you back. You are meant for more!

Freedom in the unknown: You don't need to have all the steps figured out on your path. When you experience failures, remember that a failure is just the next step toward success. You will learn more about your journey with each faith-step that appears. Also, it's fine for your business to evolve; as we move toward improved versions of ourselves, our interests may shift and expand.

Summary—"Let it go!": Be open and let go of control, go with the flow, step out in faith, let go of the fear, let go and let God lead you, know that your soul knows what you need, trust and listen to your intuition. You have the COMPLETE ability to do this!

What it Means to Be a Heart-Centered Healer in Health Care

Being a heart-centered healer in health care means I get to use my God-given gifts, intuition, and passions to help people heal in a unique way. A "pill for every ill" is not a fix but a Band-Aid. Looking at the mind, body, and spirit is vital; if one is sick, it throws the others off balance. Examining beyond the physical manifestation of disease can bring healing to the mind and body and harmony to the soul.

CONCLUSION

You've heard from these incredible, brilliant women pharmacists, and now it's your turn to take action. None of us can do this alone! We need each other to lean on for support and a loving community. It's amazing what can happen when you open yourself up to connecting with others.

Many of the women in this group and in my communities have supported each other through collaborating on various projects like retreats, Facebook or Instagram Lives, programs, and more. Reach out to these women and connect, collaborate, and join our community!

It's allowed to be EASY, and it's YOUR time to SHINE, Queen!

INTEGRATING THIS INTO YOUR LIFE

Now that you've gotten some insight on the concepts behind scaling your heart-centered business, you might be wondering how this work will help you transform your life and business.

I want you to think back to a time when you were given a strategy to follow. Perhaps it was a webinar, a free training, or a diet.

The strategy may have been on point, but you got in the way. The "head trash," the lack of follow through, and self-doubt sabotaged you.

What if that were gone?

What if you had the method and mindset to wake up every day feeling sexy, confident, worthy, and lit up about what you were creating in your life?

What if you were able to be resilient and navigate life's curveballs, while remaining focused on that big vision?

That is what this inner transformation work will give you.

Freedom, focus, and fulfillment to embody the highest version of yourself to create the life you deserve.

The work I do with women in my one-on-one sessions and in my programs, retreats, and courses combines both inner shifts and practical strategies so you are stretching yourself to your next level, while also feeling energetically aligned and scaling your profitable business.

What other Queens are saying about my coaching:

"I sold my first high-ticket $8k program!"

"It's hard not to feel inspired and motivated when you're working with Christina.

"I have known Christina for over a year now, and looking back to where I was, I am in awe of how far I've come in terms of personal and business development. After doing some of her self-paced courses and meditations and attending retreats, it was a no-brainer for me to join Step into Your Queen: Elevate Entrepreneur Academy!

"To be in Christina's energy is to be wrapped in gentle loving but direct and guiding support. EEA has you thinking outside of the box to tap into your unique gifts, show the Universe why you are worthy of abundance and understand how you are truly supported, while navigating blocks and self-sabotage with ease and flow.

"After joining Step into Your Queen: Elevate Entrepreneur Academy, I finally understood the value that I give to my clients and sold my first high-ticket $8k program!

"I am so thankful I invested in myself because now I can show up confidently and authentically in my business."

– **Katie Wood**, Pharmacist, Health Coach, and Fertility Expert

***

"I had my first 5-figure launch!"

"For those who are curious, I wanted to share my real world results from working with Christina. I was completely stuck in my business and had a block around promoting the business and myself. I did not know that I had a subconscious block (because it was subconscious), but after a year and a half of virtually zero results in my business, I was ready to try things that were outside of the 'norm' and my comfort zone.

"I attended the Elevate retreat, joined the Elevate program, hired Christina as my 1:1 coach, and finally discovered my subconscious blocks that were holding me back. I faced off with the lies I had believed about myself. Results? Prior to my work with Christina I had launches that made $0–1K (some total flops and some limited success). I've had two launches since then—the first one when I had only done limited work and had a $3k launch and the next one post-retreat where I had my first five-figure launch.

"Christina is a gem and has found her calling in helping others to rise."

– **Catherine Henderson**, Pharmacist and Health Coach

***

"I am already reaping the rewards of this new heart-centered approach after only being in Elevate Entrepreneur for ONE month!"

"I found Dr. Christina totally by chance, and I can honestly say that my life will never be the same. It was as if the Universe opened up and she appeared just when I needed a transformation coach the most! I'm currently enrolled in Christina's Elevated Entrepreneur Academy, and I'm already clearing many of the subconscious blocks that have been holding me back in my business.

"Through the detailed foundational trainings, modules, meditations, live group calls, and the Facebook group, I am gaining a whole new perspective on my business and my life.

Instead of hiding from the spotlight, I'm publicly opening up my heart to my clients and introducing them to the real me. As I am beginning to feel safe doing this, I'm already reaping the rewards of my heart-centered approach. If you're ready to step up and do the inner work necessary to up-level your business, you need to call Dr. Christina. Prepare to be amazed because she will not disappoint!"

– Kristy Redmon, Pharmacist and CEO of Windy Hill Hemp

***

"I joined Elevate, did the first few exercises on my money mindset, and got a $2,500 client paid in full within the first week!"

"Christina has helped me tremendously to unlock things in me that helped me shine my light and show up in my business with more power and visibility!

"There are no words to describe how transformative she is, and I am so grateful for her gifts!"

– **Jenna Carmichael**, PharmD

***

"Christina has helped me connect more to myself and not suppress my feelings. After attending her Elevate Retreat and working with her, I've been able to uncover more self-love and compassion for myself.

"Her work is truly life-changing, and the work we've done together has had such a big impact in my business! I am now way more connected to my heart!

– **Kimber Boothe**, PharmD

***

"Investing in MYSELF has never come easy for me. After working with Dr. Christina for over a year, I understood she does not sugar coat her love, guidance, support, strength, or willingness to stand for her clients. Recently, I was finally ready to say YES to investing in myself, and I joined Elevate Entrepreneur quickly, knowing the investment in the program would reward me financially in the future. Through EEA, my confidence in speaking with potential clients has expanded, therefor boosting my monthly gain. My personal and professional relationships have deepened, and **I was able to sign on two new partners and guide them to earn a $100 bonus and 5% commission!** The 1:1 session with Dr. Christina highlighted the direction of my message so I can create my first signature offer soon! I highly recommend working with Christina!"

– Melissa Hetrick – Pharmacist

***

Here's the thing . . .

When you are up-leveling and stretching your comfort zone edges, you need support.

Accountability, strategy, inner shifts, and surrounding yourself with other women who want to see you shine are essential ingredients for success.

If you're feeling excited as you read this book and want to dive in right away, I'd like to invite you to join the **Monetize Your Magic** private Facebook group here— https://bit.ly/monetizeyourmagicgroup.

You'll get access to exclusive trainings from me, support, community with other powerful women, and opportunities to work with me in a private 1:1 or group setting.

If you already know you're ready to dive into working together, **head to the QR code at the end of this chapter to learn more and join Step into Your Queen: Elevate Entrepreneur Academy.** This is a game-changing six-month journey that will guide you through releasing blocks, owning your brilliance, and monetizing your gifts so you can scale your profitable heart-centered business. You'll be connected with other pharmacist entrepreneurs on their big business growth journey!

These are some of the fundamental principles we dive deep into in Step into Your Queen: Elevate Entrepreneur Academy –

#1. Unlocking your gifts + owning your brilliance – This involves being able to own all parts of you – your story, mistakes/challenges, your shadows, and the authentic YOU. This isn't about perfection – it's about EMPOWERMENT and the deeper levels of self-love that are foundational if you want to scale.

#2. Unwinding unworthiness – I found that many healers in health care have patterns of unworthiness and the fear of receiving for their gifts. When I observed coaches I'd worked with who were making multiple six figures or seven figures per year, I saw that they were neutral with money. Shifting your relationship with money involves coming to a place of neutrality with money, without all of the stories, money drama, and programming about what you're able to have and opening your money channels to expand your receiving capacity.

#3. Recalibrating the masculine TO expand RECEIVING – We are often programmed to work hard to achieve results, overriding our needs or feelings in the process. One of the most common ways this manifests is through control patterns where you are operating from disempowered masculine programming—forcing, pushing, perfectionism—to create the outcomes you seek. When you hold these energetic patterns in your field, your energy is contracted, and your ability to receive is severely diminished, as was shown in David Hawkins's chart.

The old paradigm of HARD WORK = RESULTS shifts when you tap into your feminine DESIRES and take action from DECISION. This is a completely new way of operating in your business that allows for more ease and flow as you expand your receiving capacity to hold higher levels of clients and wealth.

#4. Rewiring your subconscious self-image – We often have a built-up identity tied to how we've seen ourselves our entire life. We also pick up how others have traditionally mirrored back to us how they see us. To embody your new elevated identity as a full-time entrepreneur, it requires you to rewire your subconscious self-image.

#5. Structures, systems, and support – To scale a profitable healing business, you need these three empowered masculine entities to hold higher levels of wealth and clients.

Hover over the QR code below with your Camera app to learn more about **Step into Your Queen: Elevate Entrepreneur Academy.**

Whatever your soul work is, I'll help you release blocks, own your brilliance, and own your power as a dynamic leader.

I look forward to building our connection, and I am excited for your next level!

With love + gratitude,

Christina

WORKS CITED

Chapter 06: Energetic Communication. n.d.
    https://www.heartmath.org/research/science-of-the-heart/energetic-
    communication/.

Dispenza, Joe. *Breaking the Habit of Being Yourself: How to Lose Your Mind
    and Create a New One.* Hay House, 2012.

Dr. Masaru Emoto and Water Consciousness. n.d.
    https://thewellnessenterprise.com/emoto/ (accessed May 5, 2022).

Elizabeth H. Padgett, PharmD Candidate 2020 Auburn University Harrison
    School of Pharmacy Auburn. *Pharmacist Burnout and Stress.* May 15,
    2020. https://www.uspharmacist.com/article/pharmacist-burnout-and-
    stress.

Lord, Sarah Peregrine, et al. *"More than Reflections: Empathy in Motivational
    Interviewing Includes Language Style Synchrony between Therapist
    and Client.".* May 2015.
    https://www.ncbi.nlm.nih.gov/pmc/articles/PMC5018199/.

Martin, Leslie R. et al. "The Challenge of Patient Adherence." *Therapeutics and
    Clinical Risk Management.* Dove Medical Press , Sept 2005.

ABOUT THE AUTHOR

Dr. Christina Tarantola Fontana, PharmD, CHC, CHt, is a former pharmacist, world class healer, intuitive/rapid transformation business coach, author, and hypnotist. She blends hypnotherapy, quantum physics, spirituality, and intuitive coaching to help visionary healers in health care release blocks so they can own their brilliance and scale their heart-centered business.

She's the creator of The Step into Your Queen: Elevate Entrepreneur Academy™ that helps healers in health care transform from healthcare worker to full-time entrepreneur scaling their profitable business with ease and flow.

For the last 10 years, Dr. Christina has been providing uplifting, transformational content through her YouTube videos, articles, books, and her podcast, She Rises into Desire Podcast.

For more information about Dr. Christina's programs and how she can help you impact more people with your soul gifts, please visit www.pharmacistcoach.com or contact her at christina@pharmacistcoach.com.

Made in the USA
Columbia, SC
12 October 2022

69059761R10122